IN DEFENCE OF
COPYRIGHT

IN DEFENCE OF COPYRIGHT

HUGH STEPHENS

Cormorant Books

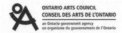

We acknowledge financial support for our publishing activities: the
Government of Canada, through the Canada Book Fund and The Canada
Council for the Arts; the Government of Ontario, through the Ontario Arts
Council, Ontario Creates, and the Ontario Book Publishing Tax Credit.
We acknowledge additional funding provided by the Government of Ontario
and the Ontario Arts Council to address the adverse effects of
the novel coronavirus pandemic.

LIBRARY AND ARCHIVES CANADA CATALOGUING IN PUBLICATION

Title: In defence of copyright / Hugh Stephens.
Names: Stephens, Hugh (Author of In defence of copyright), author.
Identifiers: Canadiana (print) 20220263930 | Canadiana (ebook) 20220284040
| ISBN 9781770866799 (softcover) | ISBN 9781770866805 (HTML)
Subjects: LCSH: Copyright—Canada. | LCSH: Copyright—Canada—History.
Classification: LCC KE2799 .S74 2022 | LCC KF2995 .S74 2022 kfmod |
DDC 346.7104/82—dc23

Cover design: Angel Guerra
Interior text design: Marijke Friesen
Manufactured by Houghton Boston in Saskatoon,
Saskatchewan in May, 2023.

Printed using paper from a responsible and sustainable resource,
including a mix of virgin fibres and recycled materials.

Printed and bound in Canada.

CORMORANT BOOKS INC.
260 ISHPADINAA (SPADINA) AVENUE, SUITE 502,
TKARONTO (TORONTO), ON M5T 2E4
www.cormorantbooks.com

TABLE OF CONTENTS

This book is dedicated to my wife, Catherine, who has travelled the world with me, always provided support, and given me the freedom to write this book, and to my daughters Nicola and Phoebe who have inspired me with their determination to achieve their goals in life.

PROLOGUE

IT IS A sad commentary on today's state of affairs that there is a need for a book defending copyright. The general public, in Canada and elsewhere, has only a vague knowledge of what copyright actually is, how it functions, and why it is needed. There are deep knowledge gaps and a prevailing impression that anything available on the internet is effectively free for the taking. If it isn't free, the view is that it should be and that copyright is not just *a* barrier but *the* barrier preventing this. Ask many librarians — who should know better — and they will say that copyright locks up content and stops it from being made available to the public. Many members of the public have heard of intellectual property but get copyright, patents, and trademarks confused. The confusion is understandable given the paucity of information available and the proclivity of even the mainstream media to frequently conflate the different forms of intellectual property protection.

My own awareness of copyright and intellectual property came slowly. After almost thirty years in the Canadian foreign service, in 2001 I had a career change and accepted a position as Senior Vice President (Public Policy) for Asia for the U.S. media conglomerate Time Warner. This necessarily entailed a greater familiarity with copyright issues than I had previously needed, given that the bread and butter of a company like Time Warner was content. Without content, the company was largely an empty shell, and the way in which its content was protected and monetized was largely through copyright. Therefore, the level of copyright protection — or the corresponding lack of it — in terms of legislation and enforcement in the countries in my region were of prime importance. As a senior representative of the company, my task was to use public policy to get governments in the region to improve their copyright regimes and to take more action to combat piracy in both its physical and digital forms.

I became aware of how little thought was given generally to intellectual property protection in many Asian countries. In most countries, the problem was not so much with the laws themselves as with the interpretation and enforcement of those laws, as well as the attitude of a public that considered theft of intellectual property, particularly copyright piracy, to not be a serious offence — perhaps not a crime at all. Today, I think people are somewhat more aware of the consequences of patent theft, but theft of copyrighted materials and trademark violations are considered by many to be more an irritant than a crime. I confess that a number of years ago when I lived in Seoul, South Korea, one of the family's weekend delights was to go down to Itaewan, the street full of vendors of knockoff goods, music, movies, and so on that was adjacent to the U.S. military base at Yongsan. Knockoff goods that closely resembled the real thing could be purchased for a fraction of the price of the genuine article. Pirated and counterfeit goods were openly displayed. The Seoul police were not interested in stopping foreigners from purchasing knockoffs that resembled genuine brand-name foreign products, a process that would result in putting some of their countrymen out of business. I am not proud of it now, but back in the late 1980s, the acquisition of bargains, even though they were clearly copyright or trademark infringing, was considered a normal weekend activity. We knew they weren't the real thing, but who cared?

This same double standard was on display a few years later when the American Women's Club of Shanghai ran a feature in its weekly newsletter informing newcomers of the best places to buy counterfeit and pirated goods. Some of those families were affiliated with either the U.S. Consulate or U.S. companies trying to protect their intellectual property in China. The U.S. government found it somewhat embarrassing, to say the least, to be lobbying the Shanghai government to close the pirate markets while dependents of consulate staff were promoting the attractions of such venues. In the end, the message was delivered to the Women's Club, and its awareness was enhanced. I have undergone the same education. Sharing this experience and helping to shape awareness of the role of copyright in society today is one way of making up for some the lapses of my earlier, unaware self.

As I hope you will come to appreciate, copyright protection is essential to promote and preserve the cultural life of the societies in which we live. There can be debates over how much protection is appropriate, but the essence of providing creators (authors, artists, sculptors, photographers, musicians, songwriters, performers, composers, filmmakers, architects, knitting pattern designers, tattoo artists, even writers of software programs) with the exclusive right to control and license reproduction and distribution of their work is what makes artistic creation viable. It is the fuel that allows the machine to run. The simplicity of establishing copyright is what makes it unique among other forms of intellectual property, although there is no shortage of legal interpretation of what is and is not protectable. The bundle of rights that constitutes copyright is not absolute; it is subject to limitations and exceptions. What these rights are, and how they apply, is the subject of Chapter 1.

Copyright did not just spring wholly formed from the mind of lawmakers. It underwent centuries of development and continues to evolve today, in the digital age. I explore some of the historical roots of copyright early in the book to set the context for the system we have today. This constitutes Chapter 2.

In some countries, such as Canada, the exceptions to copyright are considered user rights, and I have devoted

Chapter 3 to a discussion of these. At the same time, user rights need to be balanced against the moral and economic rights of those who created the works in the first place. There is a great deal of debate over the application of these exceptions and limitations; over the years, courts have interpreted where those limits lie. New circumstances and new interpretations are part of the regular ebb and flow of copyright. Some of the legal but unauthorized (by authors[1]) uses are controversial and have created major challenges for copyright holders. Finding the right balance is an ongoing challenge. I examine some of these challenges in Chapter 6.

Throughout history, there have been those who objected to the limited monopoly conferred by copyright. Their solution was to change or ignore the law. Pirated print editions actually predate copyright, and piracy has taken on new dimensions as technology has changed. Piracy, its origins, its different manifestations, its costs, and ways of dealing with it are explored in Chapters 4 and 5.

Copyright in the digital age presents new challenges, but the basic precepts can be adapted to today's environment. This is particularly important as artificial intelligence (AI) becomes part of the creative landscape. Can a work created by AI be subject to copyright protection? How does the development of AI tools affect copyright holders? These issues are covered in Chapter 7.

---

1 Often, when I use the term *author*, I am using a broad definition of the word to include all creators, not just writers. In other cases, which I hope I have made clear, I am referring to authors of books only.

Canada is but one of 181 members (at the time of print) of the Berne Convention, the international treaty that regulates copyright standards. Many of the challenges faced in Canada are reflective of the issues being grappled with in other jurisdictions. Others are a result of Canada's own experience, legal interpretations, and history of copyright. Throughout the book, I have tried to situate Canada's experience with copyright in the context of the broader international picture. Copyright in Canada has been subject to many influences: British law, American practices, French traditions, and our own unique experiences. The current state of copyright in Canada reflects all these influences.

In Chapter 8, I provide my summary defence of copyright. It is important to get it right if we are to protect our cultural sovereignty and stay innovative and creative as a nation. There is no doubt that copyright and broader concepts of intellectual property are under attack today, both from new technologies and from a misplaced belief that copyright is an obstacle to the propagation of knowledge. There are some who argue that we are entering an era that will see the end of intellectual property.[2] It is hard to take such a prognosis seriously. Copyright has adapted to technological change over many decades. The principles of copyright are as applicable in the digital world as they were in the day of physical typesetting. In a globalized

2   Adrian Johns, *Piracy: The Intellectual Property Wars from Gutenberg to Gates*, Chicago and London, University of Chicago Press, pp. 508–518.

world, with almost instantaneous communication and wide access to knowledge in various formats, a robust system of copyright is essential to ensure the continued production of and investment in quality content for the benefit and general welfare of society. Rather than preventing access to knowledge, the essence of copyright is that it encourages and facilitates creation and distribution. And if, for whatever reason, an author does not wish their work to be propagated, they surely should have the ability to exercise that right.

Finally, as a dessert offering after the main course, I have included a selection of weird and wonderful copyright stories drawn from a weekly blog on international copyright issues that I have been writing for the past six years. They illustrate some of the bizarre ways in which copyright can intersect with daily life, in the process becoming a matter of considerable jurisprudence.

I hope you will enjoy the journey and, if nothing else, come away from reading this book with a better appreciation of the role that copyright plays in contemporary society and why, in my view, respect for copyright and creators is essential if we are to protect and nourish the creative impulses of our cultural community and cultural industries.

CHAPTER I

What Is Copyright?
The Role of the Author

AS MAY SEEM obvious from its name, copyright involves the right to make copies, but today it is about much more than just reproduction. The corresponding term in French is *droit d'auteur* (author's rights), a much more complete description that captures the bundle of rights that come with copyright. Thinking of an author as a creator further broadens the definition, encompassing the many forms of expression that are captured by copyright. Creators range from writers and visual artists to musicians, performers, photographers, composers, choreographers, filmmakers, writers of software code, architects, sculptors, and, yes, even tattoo artists. The author or creator is always the first owner of copyright in the work, unless they have created the work as part of their employment or, in the United States, as a contractor producing a work for hire.

Copyright and droit d'auteur sprang from different traditions. The English common-law interpretation was based on a concept of limited economic monopolies balanced against the rights of others, such as users or competitors. Its basis was the use of economic incentives to encourage the production of works for the benefit of society. The concept of droit d'auteur is rooted in the traditional romantic view of the cultural integrity of authorship and creativity, the right of the author to control their work. Both were initially rooted in literature, and thus the right of reproduction was a key element. Over the years, however, more areas of expression and more rights have been added to copyright. The process continues today, for example, with discussions as to whether short-term copyright protection, often called neighbouring rights or ancillary rights, should be accorded to newspaper publishers to protect (for a limited time) news content they have produced. The European Union has taken such a step.

A BUNDLE OF RIGHTS

As described succinctly by the Canadian Intellectual Property Office,[1] copyright gives a copyright owner the right:

- to first distribute an unpublished work and make copies of it (or a substantial part of it) and make it available to the public
- to reproduce the work in any material form (e.g., make a shorter version, translate, adapt)

1   https://www.ic.gc.ca/eic/site/cipointernet-internetopic.nsf/eng/wr04884. html#rights; accessed January 29, 2022.

- to perform the work in public
- to communicate the work to the public by telecommunication
- to exhibit an artistic work in public

This broad description of a copyright owner's rights is underpinned by copyright legislation. The rights accorded to copyright holders in law fall into two broad categories: economic and moral.

Economic rights provide the means by which authors can authorize or exclude users of their works. Normally, this is done by either selling (assigning) or licensing the rights, often subject to some contractual limitations. This involves some form of payment for access to copyrighted material, which in turn provides the economic incentive that allows writers to write, artists to paint or draw, composers to compose, and so on. Authorization can also be provided free of charge if the copyright holder wishes to do so, with the authorization often subject to some form of limitation such as non-commercial use.

Taken together, the various rights bundled under copyright provide creators with the means to earn a living from their works and the incentive to produce more works for the benefit of society and the enjoyment of consumers.

What are these economic rights, and how do they sustain creativity?

ECONOMIC RIGHTS

First, and arguably most important, is the reproduction right, the sole right to "produce or reproduce the work or any substantial part thereof in any material form whatever...."[2]

The law establishes that it is the author who has the right to create a work and bring it into being in a tangible form. The term "any material form whatever" means that the work can be printed, written, silkscreened, filmed, or produced in a digital format. It could be carved in wood or etched in metal.

The reproduction right allows the copyright holder to exercise copyright over a "substantial part" of the work. The question of what constitutes a substantial part can be subject to judicial interpretation if an unauthorized use is challenged in court. "Substantial" could be defined by the amount of the work used, or it could be defined qualitatively if the essence of the work was used. For example, in one famous American case, the copying of one minute and fifteen seconds of a seventy-two-minute Charlie Chaplin film was considered substantial and was not permitted as a fair use.[3]

---

2 Copyright Act, Canada, (R.S.C. 1985 c.C-42); Section 3 (1).

3 Roy Export v CBS. The case involved the broadcast by CBS of a compilation of clips from Charlie Chaplin films at the time of Chaplin's death in 1977. Roy Export owned the rights to some of the films and had denied CBS the right to use certain excerpts because it was producing its own memorial to Chaplin. CBS chose to incorporate the clips anyway. Roy Export sued. CBS argued various defences, including fair use, one element of which was the amount of material used. CBS argued its use was insubstantial. It used one minute and forty-five seconds from *City*

A second right is the right of public performance. The author could, of course, perform the work themselves (reading a play or singing a song they'd composed), but often the copyright holder will authorize a public performance by someone else. In the case of music, the performing right is the right to perform a song or composition in public. An example would be a live performance, a radio or TV broadcast, streaming, or background music at a bar or restaurant. Broadcast performances are covered by a related public performance right regarding telecommunication to the public. This right relates only to public performances, but any performance outside a household setting will normally be considered public, even if no admission is charged. Thus, performing a play or showing a film at a community centre or by a church group would require copyright clearance in the form of a public performance licence.

Another key right is the right of publication. This gives the copyright holder the exclusive right to first publish a work. If you have written your first great novel but are

---

Lights (running time one hour and twenty minutes), three minutes and forty-five seconds from *The Kid* (running time one hour), fifty-five seconds from *Modern Times* (running time one hour and twenty-nine minutes), and one minute and fifteen seconds from *The Gold Rush*. The total time of the unauthorized clips used was less than seven minutes. However, the court ruled that CBS had taken the best scenes from each film and that the taking was substantial. CBS lost the case on this and other grounds. Roy Export Etc. v Columbia Broadcasting System, 503 F. Supp. 1137 (S.D.N.Y. 1980); https://law.justia.com/cases/federal/district-courts/ FSupp/503/1137/1466752/; accessed January 29, 2022.

not yet ready to expose it to the world, it is your call as to whether it gets published or remains forever unfinished on your computer. Incidentally, if you send it by computer to someone to read, that does not constitute publication. Once an author has published a work, however, they have no rights over resales,[4] although in many countries artists do get a share of the proceeds of subsequent sales if their artwork is sold by auction houses or dealers. This is known as the artists' resale right. Some have argued that the same principle should apply to book authors, but this would be very complex and costly to administer. In Canada, however, writers do get revenues from the Public Lending Right Program, according to a formula that gives them revenues depending on whether their works are present on the shelves of surveyed public libraries.[5] Which

4 In the United States, this is referred to as the first sale doctrine. Once a book is sold, the owner can resell it without recourse to the copyright owner. However, an owner cannot reproduce the work without permission. In the case of e-books, in most instances the reader is not buying a copy of the work but simply obtaining a licence to use it, subject to certain conditions. As with hard copies, an e-book cannot be reproduced without permission.

5 The Canadian Public Lending Right Program was instituted in 1986 and was the result of concerns at the time by authors that they were being ripped off by libraries. But not every book loaned out is a forgone sale, a point repeatedly made by librarians. More than thirty countries have a public lending right. In Canada, it is administered by the Canada Council for the Arts and is funded by the federal government. Book authors are required to register their titles. Seven marker libraries are used to determine the inventory of books that will receive remuneration. The average payout per author is normally under $1,000 annually, with a maximum payment to an individual author of $4,500.

actions constitute publication vary. A performance of a work does not constitute publication, but the construction of an architectural work does.

Flowing from the right of publication is a series of related rights, such as the right of adaptation, the right of translation, and the right of retransmission. In the case of a dramatic work, the right of adaptation gives the author the right to convert it, or to authorize its conversion, into a novel or other non-dramatic work. In the case of a novel or other non-dramatic work, or of an artistic work, it confers the reverse right to convert it into a dramatic work, such as a play, opera, or film. The nature of the translation right is obvious. The copyright holder has the exclusive right to translate or to authorize others to translate the work into any language from the original. The retransmission right relates to television broadcasts, where content that was initially authorized by copyright holders as a telecommunication to the public is retransmitted through a satellite or cable system. A royalty is payable for such retransmissions, normally through a collecting society (discussed below).

The right to make available is exactly as described. It means that content is made available to the public, but the public needs to take some action in order to access the material. For example, content is made available for downloading or streaming in a way that allows a member of the public to have access to it from a place and at a time individually chosen by that person.

All these rights are underpinned by the right of authorization, which gives the author or copyright holder the exclusive right to authorize use. No one else can substitute for the copyright owner, although sometimes compulsory licences are issued by governments. In these cases, even if a copyright holder did not wish to issue a licence for use, they cannot withhold permission. Retransmission of distant television signals (those signals not capable of being received over the air) is an example of a situation where a compulsory licence is issued.

Copyright holders also have the right to block the importation of infringing works, normally books, through obtaining a court order and applying to customs authorities to prohibit import.

There are several economic rights that apply to specific types of copyrighted works, such as artistic works, sound recordings, and computer programs. The exhibition right gives artists the right to present at a public exhibition (other than displaying for sale or hire). This means that an owner of a painting must obtain the permission of the artist to exhibit the work publicly, such as in an art gallery or museum. It is worth remembering that even if you purchase a painting or other work of art, you do not own the copyright to the work. You own the physical incarnation, but you cannot reproduce it or exhibit it publicly without permission from the copyright holder.

The distribution right allows the copyright holder to sell, lend, or rent the work. A subset of distribution, the commercial rental right, gives copyright holders the ability to authorize commercial rentals of musical or audio-visual programs on DVDs (and thereby receive royalties), but given the transition from DVDs to online streaming and the closing of most rental stores, this right is not of much use today.

When it comes to sound recordings, movies, and broadcasting, there are layers of rights involved, all of which need to be respected. In the case of sound recordings, there could be separate copyright in the lyrics and the score. These are often referred to as mechanical rights. Then there are the performers, who have performing rights as musicians and singers. When music is matched to a film in the making of a motion picture or television show, there are synchronization rights involved, and permission must be obtained from the copyright holder of the musical work. (For purposes of simplification, mechanical rights refer to audio works while synchronization rights refer to video works.) Productions such as movies, television shows, and operas involve multiple rights that have to be obtained and licensed before the production can be released. Broadcasters also have rights in their broadcast transmissions.

Some rights are described slightly differently depending on the country, although most countries have established very similar rights under copyright. For example, in the United States, their law refers to the "right of public display," a term not used in Canada, although the exhibition right is similar.

MORAL RIGHTS

In addition to the bundle of economic rights that intersect and reinforce each other, copyright holders also enjoy what are called moral rights. The extent of moral rights varies from country to country and tends to be more extensive in countries that have developed their copyright regimes more on the droit d'auteur premise than on the utilitarian incentive provided by economic rights. Moral rights exist in both Canada and the United States, although not to the same extent as in many European countries. Moral rights relate to the ability of the creator to protect the integrity of their work from a reputational rather than economic perspective. They persist even after an author has assigned copyright to another person or entity. Broadly speaking, they fall into the categories of right of paternity, right of integrity, and right of association.

Paternity (not exactly a gender-neutral phrase) means the right to be identified as the author or creator of a work, but also the right to remain anonymous as it includes the right to use a pseudonym. Thus, we may never find out who the graffiti artist Banksy really is.[6] Integrity gives the author a say in how the work is used, even if the copyright has passed to someone else. This is to prevent damage to the creator through distortion, mutilation, destruction, or modification of the work. Two notable moral rights cases,

6 There are many theories as to who the anonymous British street artist really is, including speculation that he is more than one person.

one in Canada and one in the U.S., illustrate the nature of moral rights and the right of integrity.

The first is the case of Canadian artist Michael Snow's flying geese. Snow's work "Flight Stop," a representation of sixty geese, hangs in the main galleria of the Eaton Centre in downtown Toronto. Commissioned by the centre's developers in 1979, the geese became entangled in a legal controversy over Snow's moral rights in 1982. Just before Christmas of that year, the management of the centre decided to bedeck Snow's geese with red ribbons and use photos of the decorated geese on promotional items. Snow objected, claiming that the addition of the ribbons altered the character and purpose of the work and negatively affected his artistic reputation. Mall management disagreed, and the case went to the Ontario High Court (Snow v The Eaton Centre Ltd.),[7] which ruled in Snow's favour. The Eaton Centre was given three days to remove the ribbons, which they did. Snow had made his point and asserted his moral rights.

The second case relates to graffiti painted on some abandoned buildings known as 5Pointz, in New York City, and the actions taken by the buildings' owners, David and Jerry Wolkoff. Back in the 1990s, the Wolkoffs allowed some derelict factory buildings they owned and leased as artist's studios to be festooned in street art. The painted buildings

7 Snow v The Eaton Centre Ltd. (1982) 70 C.P.R. (2d) 105; https://www
.cipil.law.cam.ac.uk/virtual-museum/snow-v-eaton-centre-ltd-1982-70-
cpr-2d-105; accessed January 29, 2022.

became a tourist attraction and a magnet for a wide range of street artists. Several years later, the Wolkoffs decided they wanted to sell the property for development and tear down the buildings. A group of artists, including one who acted as curator, sought an injunction in 2013 to block the demolition, whereupon the owners whitewashed the buildings overnight, in the process destroying the art. The artists then sued the Wolkoffs under a relatively obscure piece of legislation known as the Visual Artists Rights Act (VARA) of 1990. Under that legislation, the author of a "painting, drawing, print, or sculpture, existing in a single copy or in a limited edition of two hundred or fewer, shall have the right ... to prevent any intentional distortion, mutilation, or other modification of that work which would be prejudicial to his or her honor or reputation."[8]

In the end, the court decided the buildings would have to come down, and a demolition permit was issued. That's when Jerry Wolkoff got a big surprise. The VARA lawsuit continued and in 2018, the court found in favour of the plaintiffs. The artists were awarded damages of $6.7 million for the landowner's act of destruction, even though there was no question that the Wolkoffs owned the buildings and had the legal right to demolish them. Moral rights prevailed.

---

8   17 U.S. Code § 106A - Rights of certain authors to attribution and integrity; https://www.law.cornell.edu/uscode/text/17/106A; accessed January 29, 2022.

The right of association is another right that gives an artist or author the right to prevent use of a work in association with a product, service, cause, or institution. An animal rights campaigner might not like their work used to promote the sale of sausages. On occasion, musicians object to political campaigns using their work to promote political objectives, although strictly speaking this usually relates to unlicensed use of copyrighted material rather than moral rights. Numerous musicians objected to the use of their music during Donald Trump's 2016 and 2020 campaigns even though, in some instances, the Trump campaign had legally licensed use of the music.[9]

OTHER RIGHTS

There are other rights associated with copyright that may not be incorporated specifically in copyright law but that relate to copyright. They may be included in the laws of some countries or some U.S. states but not others. I have already discussed the public lending right and the artists' resale right. Another right is known as the personality right or publicity right. This allows individuals to control the commercial use of their identity, such as name, image, likeness, or other identifiers. It could be invoked by well-known personalities who do not wish to appear to endorse certain products by having their image associated with that product.

9 Among musicians reported to have objected were Neil Young, the Beatles, Bruce Springsteen, CCR, Elton John, Guns N' Roses, Leonard Cohen's estate, Pavarotti's estate, Nickelback, Pharrell Williams, Prince, Queen, and the Rolling Stones.

Other rights relate to a performer's performance, rather than simply performance rights. This protects a performer from having their performance recorded or broadcast without permission.

There are also rights known as neighbouring rights (i.e., rights that are adjacent to copyright). These include royalties paid by radio stations to collecting societies representing performers and record labels. Collecting societies, or collectives, are associations that represent groups of copyright holders who would not by themselves have the means to track usage and collect royalties for reproduction of their works. Copyright collectives exist in several domains: publishing, music, and fine arts. A more recent form of neighbouring right relates to the rights conferred on media outlets (newspapers and magazines) in the European Union, enabling them to negotiate with internet platforms that have been excerpting some of their news coverage. News is generally not subject to copyright, but the new publishing right for media outlets in the EU gives content producers the right to control the commercial use of their news coverage for two years after publication.

DURATION OF COPYRIGHT

The limited period for protection of news content contrasts with the much more robust period of copyright protection afforded most forms of creativity. This is understandable, since news coverage is relatively ephemeral and loses its utility and resale value quickly. The minimum term of protection for most works protected by copyright under the terms of the Berne Convention is the life of the author plus fifty years, [10] although many countries have adopted an extended term of life of the author plus seventy years. If an author produced a successful work early in their career and lived a long life, copyright could well exceed a century. For some works, such as sound recordings, where there is no single author, the term of copyright protection starts from the date of recording (referred to as fixation) rather than anyone's death. The same principle also exists generally in the case of motion pictures.

Some commentators argue that the term of copyright protection is too long, especially now that many countries are extending their term of protection. The case for longer terms has two basic arguments: first, it allows an author to provide for their heirs and estate; and second, it provides an additional economic incentive for production and distribution since the extra period of protection allows for a longer period to recoup investment in a work. For example, the cost of making a movie from a book or script can be enormous, requiring the recapture of the investment

10 The Berne Convention is an international treaty first signed by several countries in 1886, providing reciprocal protection for copyrighted works. Over the years, its coverage has expanded, and many more countries have acceded to the convention, including, in 1989, the United States. Canada became a member of the Berne Convention upon its establishment because at that time it was part of the British Empire, and Britain's accession included its colonies and territories. Canada acceded in its own right in 1928. Today, 181 member states have acceded to Berne.

over many years through licensing of the content in various formats such as theatrical release, pay-per-view, television syndication, streaming, DVD sales, and so on. In other words, it makes the sale or licensing of the rights more valuable and brings greater return to the author or their estate in the form of extended royalties. It also protects the considerable investment in the development of copyrighted content by corporate entities, ultimately helping to ensure the creation of new content for the benefit of audiences.

USER RIGHTS AND EXCEPTIONS

So far, we have discussed the rights of copyright owners. These rights are balanced by many limitations and exceptions to copyright allowing users limited, specified uses without authorization from or payment to the copyright holder. In the United States, this is known as the fair use doctrine. Fair use can be used as a defence against claims of unauthorized use. In Canada and most other countries, exceptions are more precisely defined under what is known as fair dealing, although the Supreme Court of Canada has declared fair dealing exceptions to be user rights rather than just a defence against infringement. User rights and exceptions are dealt with in Chapter 3.

THE PURPOSE OF COPYRIGHT

Copyright, a limited form of property protection, exists not just for the immediate benefit of the creator but more widely for the benefit of society. As we will see in Chapter 2, the rationale for the first copyright laws was to promote learning. Noted copyright scholar Jane C. Ginsberg said, "Copyright law secures human creativity in works of authorship. Enforceable authorial property rights advance the public interest by promoting an ecosystem of authorship: a robust copyright environment encourages authors to create works that inform and enrich the polity, and from which other authors may draw ideas, information and reasonable amounts of protected expression in their own authorial endeavors. Copyright promotes artistic freedom and free speech by enabling authors to earn a living from their creativity ... Copyright thus promotes a diversity of expressions that might otherwise remain unvoiced."[11]

SUMMARY
This chapter reviews the bundle of rights that constitute copyright protection for authors and differentiates between economic and moral rights. Economic rights developed primarily in common law and were based on the utilitarian model of providing an incentive to encourage the production of more works for the benefit of society. Moral rights relate more to the continental tradition of droit d'auteur, the natural property right conferred on creators.

11 Ginsburg, Jane C., Overview of Copyright Law (July 1, 2016). Forthcoming, Oxford Handbook of Intellectual Property, Rochelle Dreyfuss & Justine Pila, Eds., Columbia Public Law Research Paper No. 14-518, Available at SSRN: https://ssrn.com/abstract=2811179; accessed January 29, 2022.

The various types of rights are discussed, including newer rights that have been added as technology has changed. User rights, which will be discussed in greater depth in Chapter 3, are touched on.

CHAPTER 2

The Historical Roots
of Copyright

MOST SCHOLARS CONSIDER modern copyright to be rooted in the 1710 British law known as the Statute of Anne (also known as the Copyright Act of 1710). The law was titled "An Act for the Encouragement of Learning, by Vesting the Copies of Printed Books in the Authors or Purchasers of Copies, during the Times therein mentioned."[1] Its purpose was clearly outlined in its preamble:

> Whereas Printers, Booksellers, and other Persons, have of late frequently taken the Liberty of Printing, Reprinting, and Publishing, or causing to be Printed, Reprinted, and Published Books, and other Writings, without the Consent of the Authors or Proprietors of such Books and Writings, to their very great Detriment, and too often to the Ruin of them and their Families: For Preventing therefore such Practices for the future, and for the Encouragement of

1 8 Anne. c. 21.

Learned Men to Compose and Write useful Books; May it please Your Majesty, that it may be Enacted ...[2]

The law granted authors protection for new works for fourteen years provided that the work was registered with the Stationers' Company in London and copies "on the best paper" were deposited with various universities in England and Scotland. The term of protection could be renewed for a further fourteen years if the author was still living at the time the original term expired. (It also gave twenty-one years of protection to publishers who already had books in print at the time of enactment.) Infringers could be fined one penny per page, a considerable sum in those days, with the author and the Crown sharing the proceeds. The infringing work was also to be destroyed. Noteworthy is the rationale for the legislation: "... for the Encouragement of Learned Men to Compose and Write useful Books ..."

This law was the outgrowth of a long struggle by printers in London to exercise a monopoly over the printing of various publications. Since the establishment in London in 1403 of the Stationers' Company, a guild of printers, bookbinders, booksellers, and others associated with the book trade (but, significantly, not authors), there had been various attempts to establish monopolies and licensing regimes. But the 1710 Statute of Anne empowered not

2 https://avalon.law.yale.edu/18th_century/anne_1710.asp; accessed December 18, 2021.

printers but *authors*, and gave authors (or those to whom they assigned their rights) the exclusive right to print or reprint their books. That remains the case today.

If the Statute of Anne is the source from which English copyright law springs, then Article 1, Section 8, Clause 8 of the U.S. Constitution is the wellspring for American copyright law. The Statute of Anne did not apply to the American colonies prior to the Declaration of Independence, although several of the individual colonies had their own copyright laws. Significantly, copyright was considered important enough to be included in the Constitution of the United States, concluded in 1789, making copyright a federal power. What is known as the Patent and Copyright Clause reads as follows: "[The Congress shall have power] To promote the progress of science and useful arts, by securing for limited times to authors and inventors the exclusive right to their respective writings and discoveries."

The Copyright Act of 1790 was passed to bring into effect this constitutional provision, with the duration of copyright established at fourteen years, with a possible fourteen-year extension, identical to the period of protection conferred by the Statute of Anne. The rationale was similar to that of the British statute: to promote learning (science and useful arts). These statutes are the foundation for copyright laws that have been developed not only in Britain and the United States but also in former British dominions around the world, including Canada. They have been expanded, modified, and interpreted over the years and continue to undergo modification, but they provide the fundamental underpinning of modern copyright law.

Contrary to popular belief, however, the Statute of Anne was not the first time that the legal right to reproduce a work was placed in the hands of authors rather than printers. If one digs a little deeper, there is a treasure trove of studies relating to copyright predating the Statute of Anne by at least a couple of centuries. The Republic of Venice, a centre for book publishing in the fifteenth and sixteenth centuries, was particularly active in granting a *privilegio* to certain publishers to print a particular text, preventing others from importing texts, and allowing certain bookshops to sell texts. But the privilegio was not limited to printers and publishers, although that was the most common form.

In what is considered the foundational work on the topic of Venetian printing, Horatio Brown in his 1891 opus "The Venetian Printing Press"[3] notes that in 1486, the Venetian College (Cabinet) bestowed upon one Marco Antonio Sabellico the sole right to authorize the publication of his work on the history of the republic, under penalty of a fine of five hundred ducats. Brown states that this was the first instance in which the government recognized an author's literary proprietorship of their own work. Thereafter, it was not uncommon for authors to have exclusive rights to their own works, although it was

---

3 New York, G.P. Putnams Sons, 1891 (available online at https://archive .org/details/cu31924029498445; accessed February 1. 2022.

more usual for those rights to be vested in printers. Copyright was not automatic; it had to be applied for, was not always granted, and, if granted, was usually granted to the first applicant. Other forms of copyright related to printed images, woodcuts, engravings, and etchings.

While this may be an interesting historical footnote, modern copyright law really starts with the Statute of Anne. It covered only reproduction and did not include many of the other rights now commonly associated with copyright, such as performance, distribution, or derivative rights. In the years that followed, the changes that were made to copyright fell into five main areas: the expansion of copyright from books to other forms of creative expression; the negotiation of bilateral treaties and international conventions by which copyrights in one country were respected elsewhere; the duration of copyright protection; the types of rights protected; and exceptions to copyright protection.

EXPANSION OF COPYRIGHT COVERAGE

In the beginning, literary works were protected by copyright, not just books but also pamphlets and articles. There was considerable debate as to what kinds of written work could be protected, but by the end of the nineteenth century, it was generally accepted that to enjoy protection, a work had to incorporate a degree of originality. For example, the facts of news could not be protected, nor could compilations like telephone books. Today, the World Intellectual Property Organization (WIPO), a UN agency, provides a list[4] of what can be protected by copyright. The list is wide-ranging:

- literary works such as novels, poems, plays, reference works, newspaper articles (but not the fact of news by themselves);
- computer programs, databases;
- films, musical compositions, and choreography;
- artistic works such as paintings, drawings, photographs, and sculpture;
- architecture; and
- advertisements, maps, and technical drawings.

Copyright has been extended over the years as new technologies have produced new categories of works, beginning with photography and going on to include player piano music rolls, recorded music in various formats, broadcasts, films, television programs, and computer programs. There was initial resistance to including some new forms of creativity, such as photography, which was considered by some to be a simple mechanical process devoid of creativity. It was the photographs of the U.S. Civil War by Mathew Brady, among other things, that led to photography being protected by copyright law in the United States. In March 1865, amendments were passed to the U.S. Copyright Act extending copyright protection to photographs and

4   https://www.wipo.int/copyright/en/faq_copyright.html; accessed December 15, 2021.

photographic negatives, although it was not until almost twenty years later that the United States Supreme Court upheld the amendment, ruling that photographs fell within the Copyright Clause of the U.S. Constitution.[5]

In Canada, protection of photographs goes back to 1868, when the Department of Agriculture of the new Dominion of Canada was established. Among the tasks entrusted to the Minister of Agriculture was responsibility for patents, copyright, industrial designs, and trademarks. As part of the legislation establishing the department, the Copyright Act of 1868 provided for twenty-eight years of protection for the purpose of printing, reprinting, publishing, reproducing, or vending for the author of "any book, map, chart or musical composition, or of any original painting, drawing, statuary, sculpture or photograph," as well as for prints and engravings. Protection was subject to the deposit of two copies of the work (or a written description of an artistic work or sculpture) and the payment of a registration fee of a dollar.

The issue of whether player piano rolls infringed songwriters' copyright was the subject of several high-profile lawsuits and eventually led to the establishment of mechanical licensing rights in the 1909 U.S. Copyright Act.[6]

5   https://www.copyright.gov/history/lore/pdfs/200902%20CLore
_February2009.pdf; accessed December 15, 2021.

6   http://www.zvirosen.com/2018/04/27/player-pianos-and-the
-origins-of-compulsory-licensing-some-details-of-its-origins/; accessed
December 18, 2021.

INTERNATIONAL COPYRIGHT

The first copyright laws applied only to national jurisdictions. For example, British authors were protected under Britain's copyright laws, but the works of French authors in Britain were not protected, nor were those of British authors in France or elsewhere. This led to many instances of book piracy where the works of non-national authors were freely reprinted without permission and payment. Thus, Dutch and Belgian printers specialized in printing cheap French works, and French and American publishers freely reproduced British works. While import of these pirated works for commercial sale was prohibited by the home countries, the system was leaky. Pirated copies were supposed to be confiscated at the border, but the rules were often unclear, and enforcement was lax. Even if they were somewhat protected in their home market, authors lost the potential for collecting any royalties for works printed and sold abroad.

To address this situation, various remedies were attempted. Britain passed an International Copyright Act in 1838, hoping to entice other countries into giving protection to British authors in return for reciprocal protection in Britain. Overtures were made to various countries, but there were no takers. Eventually, negotiations began among several countries with a view to reaching bilateral copyright agreements. By the early 1850s, Britain had signed reciprocal copyright treaties with both Prussia and France. France suffered from pirated printing of French works in neighbouring countries and tried to reach agreements with Switzerland, Belgium, Holland, and Germany. Eventually, France tried to seize the initiative by unilaterally offering protection in France for foreign works regardless of whether French works were protected reciprocally, with the proviso that the foreign author would only receive in France protection equivalent to that which they received at home, rather than national treatment.[7] This was intended to incentivize foreign authors to push their home authorities to negotiate bilateral treaties with France, where national treatment would be granted, and it was also in line with the French view of the natural law of property expressed in the droit d'auteur doctrine.[8]

This gap in enforcement of copyright among countries led to perverse situations. In Canada, it was common practice to import cheaper, unauthorized U.S. editions of British works rather than pay for the more expensive authorized British edition. Of course, it was illegal to import the U.S. editions into Canada (which was then part of the British Empire), but the border was long and loosely controlled. Moreover, Canadian printers naturally wanted to supply the Canadian market themselves. To do so, they would have to obtain publication rights from British authors or

7 National treatment means that a foreign national or entity receives equivalent ("no less favourable") treatment under the law as would a national of that country.

8 Catherine Seville, *The Internationalisation of Copyright Law*, Cambridge University Press, 2006, p. 57.

publishers, making it uneconomical to compete with the much cheaper pirated U.S. editions that dominated the Canadian market. One response adopted by Canadian printers was to publish unauthorized versions of American works (which was legal to do in Canada) and then sell them in the U.S. (which was not). I will explore this issue more in Chapter 3, dealing with piracy.

The hodgepodge of bilateral treaties was an unsatisfactory solution for the protection of authors' works. As a result, a movement sprang up for the adoption of a uniform international copyright law. A large international conference was held in Brussels in 1858 that included governments, libraries, literary and scientific associations, authors, artists, legal practitioners, booksellers, publishers, and printers. Nothing was resolved, but the groundwork was laid for what eventually became the Berne Convention of 1886. French novelist Victor Hugo had played a leading role in pushing for an international convention, and finally, on September 9, 1886, ten countries signed the first international convention on copyright — Belgium, France, Germany, Great Britain, Haiti, Italy, Liberia, Spain, Switzerland, and Tunisia. That is an interesting group of countries for a nineteenth-century treaty, and one wonders at the interest of Haiti, Liberia, and Tunisia. In any event, neither Haiti nor Liberia ratified the treaty, leaving just eight initial founding members. There must have been a serious case of buyer's remorse since neither Haiti nor Liberia joined the convention until more than a century later (Liberia in 1989 and Haiti in 1996). One suspects that the representatives who attended the conference and signed the convention on those countries' behalf did not have full authority to do so. Today, 181 states have acceded to Berne.

Given Canada's quasi-colonial status at the time, it, along with other components of the British Empire, became a member of Berne upon the accession of the United Kingdom. But Canada's situation was different from other parts of the Empire, and in the initial years, Canada questioned the benefits of Berne and indeed unsuccessfully petitioned the British government to allow it to withdraw.[9] Unlike the Australian colonies, it had ready access to British works printed in the United States, and it also had its own printing interests to protect. Foreign affairs and treaty making were not yet part of the powers of the young dominion, but copyright was, and on several occasions the Canadian Parliament endeavoured to pass copyright legislation that would have created a distinct Canadian copyright regime. Where Canadian legislation conflicted with British interests, it was vetoed by the governor general,[10] who at that

9   Sara Bannerman, Ph.D. Thesis Abstract, "Canada and the Berne Convention, 1886–1971," Carleton University, 2009; https://curve. carleton.ca/7a272264-6cd1-46d0-a09a-b972a5d9c2db; accessed January 5, 2022; Bannerman, "The Struggle for Canadian Copyright: Imperialism to Internationalism, 1842–1971," UBC Press, Vancouver, 2013, Chapter 5, pp. 47–68.

10   See Meera Nair, "The Geopolitics of Nineteenth-Century Canadian Copyright, as seen by some British Authors," Papers of the Bibliographical Society of Canada, Vol. 55, No. 2, 2017; https://jps.library.utoronto.ca/ index.php/bsc/article/view/32287; accessed January 5, 2022.

time was not only the representative of the Crown but also of the British government. Copyright legislation was also undergoing revision in Britain, resulting in the Imperial Copyright Act of 1911, upon which the first comprehensive Canadian legislation was based in 1921. In 1928, Canada joined Berne in its own right.

THE BERNE CONVENTION

The Berne Convention established some basic ground rules for international copyright and was based on three main principles: national treatment with minimum standards, automatic protection, and independence of protection. The principle of national treatment, a staple in trade agreements, gives foreign works no less favourable protection than domestic works in each signatory country. This is related to independence of protection, which has been interpreted to mean that a work is protected in a signatory country even if the author is from a country that provides less or no protection or is from a country that is not a member of Berne, provided that the work is published in a Berne signatory country. In other words, protection is not conditional on the degree of protection in an author's home country; protection does not have to be reciprocal.

There are some exceptions to these rules when the level of protection exceeds Berne Convention minimums. The best example is the duration of copyright protection. Berne established the minimum term of protection for individual works as the lifespan of the author plus fifty years.

Several countries, such as those of the European Union, have extended the term of protection to life of the author plus seventy years; however, the additional twenty years of protection is extended only on a reciprocal basis. In other words, works of authors from countries that provide a term of protection strictly in accordance with the Berne Convention's minimum do not enjoy the longer term of protection available in the EU.

The third principle of Berne is automatic protection.[11] In other words, there is no registration requirement to establish copyright. This makes copyright the easiest form of intellectual property to establish. A work is automatically granted protection provided it is fixed in a tangible medium and meets minimal criteria of originality. Some countries, including Canada and the United States, maintain a registration process, but it is optional. The advantage of registration is that there is a definitive record of copyright held in a central repository, although in the case of Canada, a copy of the work is no longer kept as a condition of copyright registration. However, Canadian publishers are required to provide one to two copies of each book to Library and Archives Canada under the Library and Archives of Canada Act. In the United States, registration is required for a U.S. work if legal proceedings are to be launched in cases of infringement. In a legal quirk, registration is not required for foreign works in the United States as a

---

11 Automatic protection was adopted at the Berlin Act of the Parties in 1908.

condition of bringing a legal proceeding for infringement, as non-registration is a condition of Berne. When the U.S. joined the Berne Convention in 1989, it agreed to extend Berne privileges in the United States to the nationals of all Berne Convention signatory states, but it did not change the existing rules regarding registration that applied to U.S. citizens. Thus, in this one instance, foreign works in the U.S. get better than national treatment.[12]

Although the United States did not join the Berne Convention until more than a century after its establishment, the U.S. did move shortly after the creation of Berne to recognize the copyright of non-Americans reciprocally through the adoption by Congress of the International Copyright Act of 1891, commonly known as the Chace Act.[13] Recognition of foreign works in the U.S., however, was subject to a restrictive manufacturing clause that required that two copies of the work, typeset or printed from plates, negatives, or drawings made within the U.S., be deposited at the Library of Congress. This was a sop to the U.S. printing industry designed to prevent the wholesale importation of foreign works. Therefore, foreign publishers either had to invest in having an edition of their work printed in the U.S. to enjoy copyright protection or import

12 https://www.copyright.gov/comp3/chap2000/ch2000-foreign-works .pdf; accessed January 1, 2022.

13 International Copyright Act (The Chace Act), Washington DC (1891), Primary Sources on Copyright (1450–1900), eds. L. Bently & M. Kretschmer, www.copyrighthistory.org; accessed January 1, 2022.

printed works that could be pirated. While the U.S. stayed outside Berne for many years, many U.S. publishers sought its benefits by simultaneously publishing their works in the U.S. and in a Berne Convention country. Often, that "Berne publication" took place in Canada through the Canadian subsidiary of a U.S. publishing house. This became known as the "back door to Berne."[14]

The Berne Convention has become the international standard, including its Article 2, which provides a broad definition of literary and artistic works. The definition describes a covered work as:

> every production in the literary, scientific and artistic domain, whatever may be the mode or form of its expression, such as books, pamphlets and other writings; lectures, addresses, sermons and other works of the same nature; dramatic or dramatico-musical works; choreographic works and entertainments in dumb show; musical compositions with or without words; cinematographic works to which are assimilated works expressed by a process analogous to cinematography; works of drawing, painting, architecture, sculpture, engraving and lithography; photographic works to which are assimilated works expressed by a process analogous to photography; works of applied art; illustrations, maps, plans, sketches and three-dimensional works relative to geography, topography, architecture or science.[15]

---

14 https://legal-lingo.com/back-door-to-berne; accessed January 1, 2022.

15 Berne Convention for the Protection of Literary and Artistic Works, Article 2 (1); https://wipolex.wipo.int/en/text/283698; accessed December 19, 2021.

The first line of Article 2 casts the net wide and leaves the mode and form of expression open, allowing for future technological developments with respect to forms of content fixation and delivery.

Berne requires certain minimum standards, such as definitions of what constitutes a literary and artistic work, setting life plus fifty for the duration of copyright, and granting patrimonial rights (probably more properly called "creators' rights" today.) These include the rights of reproduction, distribution, public performance, broadcasting and other communication to the public, translation, and adaption. The moral rights of paternity and integrity (discussed in Chapter 1) are also required for all signatories.

OTHER COPYRIGHT TREATIES

Berne has been modified and expanded at a number of conferences over the years, most recently in the 1970s. There are also other international conventions that deal with specific aspects of copyright law. They are administered by the World Intellectual Property Organization, established in 1967 and based in Geneva. These treaties include:

- the Rome Convention for the Protection of Performers, Producers of Phonograms and Broadcasting Organisations (1961)
- the Convention for the Protection of Producers of Phonograms Against Unauthorized Duplication of Their Phonograms (1971)

- the Brussels Convention Relating to the Distribution of Programme-Carrying Signals Transmitted by Satellite (1974)
- the WIPO Copyright Treaty (1996)
- the WIPO Performances and Phonograms Treaty (1996)
- the Beijing Treaty on Audiovisual Performances (2012)
- the Marrakesh Treaty to Facilitate Access to Published Works for Persons Who Are Blind, Visually Impaired or Otherwise Print Disabled (2013)

The names of most of these treaties are self-explanatory. The two 1996 WIPO treaties deal with protection of rights in the digital environment. The WIPO Copyright Treaty added computer programs and certain databases to categories that could be protected under copyright. It also obliges contracting parties to provide legal remedies against the circumvention of technological protection measures (e.g., encryption) used by authors in connection with the exercise of their rights, and against the removal or altering of rights management information. The WIPO Performances and Phonograms Treaty provides the same protection to performers and phonogram (recording) producers.

In addition to the specialized treaties listed above, one other international copyright convention deserves mention. This is the Universal Copyright Convention (UCC) of 1951. At the time, the United States and other countries had declined to join the Berne Convention because of the conditions that Berne imposed, particularly that grant of copyright be automatic with no requirement for registration. Countries could join both the UCC and Berne. At one point in the 1980s, there were more members of the UCC than Berne, and of the seventy-three members of the UCC, twenty-five were not members of Berne. With the accession of the United States to Berne in 1989 and the negotiation of the TRIPS agreement (see below), the UCC became increasingly irrelevant. Today, there are no members of the UCC that are not also members of Berne, and the Berne Convention has for all intents and purposes fully supplanted the UCC.[16]

TRIPS

Finally, there is the TRIPS agreement of 1994.[17] TRIPS (the Agreement on Trade-Related Aspects of Intellectual Property Rights) is part of Annex 1C of the Uruguay Round agreement establishing the World Trade Organization (WTO). TRIPS requires WTO members to comply with most elements of the Berne Convention (moral rights excepted), even if not signatories, and requires contracting parties to sign and ratify the 1996 WIPO treaties (not part of Berne). It also subjected intellectual property issues to the WTO

16 Jorgen Blomqvist, "Universal Copyright Convention-RIP," The IP Kat, December 22, 2021; https://ipkitten.blogspot.com/2021/12/guest-post-universal-copyright.html; accessed December 30, 2021.

17 https://www.wto.org/english/docs_e/legal_e/31bis_trips_01_e.htm; accessed December 19, 2021.

dispute settlement process (see Chapter 5 for the WTO dispute between Qatar and Saudi Arabia over sports broadcasting). Under the Berne Convention, if contracting states had disagreements over the application of the convention, there was no statutory means to resolve disputes.

The TRIPS agreement adopts the principle of national treatment and incorporated Berne's three-step test[18] to judge whether actions taken by governments in the area of intellectual property violate the terms of the agreement. The Berne Convention includes a provision allowing certain exceptions to copyright protection, subject to the following limitations: "It shall be a matter for legislation in the countries of the Union to permit the reproduction of such works in certain special cases, provided that such reproduction does not conflict with a normal exploitation of the work and does not unreasonably prejudice the legitimate interests of the author."[19]

The three-step test thus became the criteria by which to judge whether exceptions to copyright protection meet the requirements of TRIPS.

18 For a fuller discussion of the application of the three-step test, see Susy Frankel and Daniel J. Gervais, *Advanced Introduction to International Intellectual Property*, Cheltenham UK and Manchester, USA, Elgar, 2016, pp. 56–77.

19 Berne, Article 9 (2), https://wipolex.wipo.int/en/text/283698; accessed December 19, 2021.

IRISH MUSIC CASE

The provision to bring copyright disputes under the WTO dispute settlement process led to the so-called Irish Music Case,[20] in which the EU brought a case against the U.S. for non-payment of royalties to Irish performers for music played in certain bars and restaurants in the U.S. Normally, music played in commercial establishments must be licensed, with licence fees collected on behalf of copyright holders by what are called performing rights organizations (or collective societies in Canada). Originally, there was an exception in U.S. copyright law for small businesses playing music on the radio (think a mom-and-pop store playing music on the radio in the background). But in 1998, the U.S. Congress dropped the background radio requirement and expanded the royalty payment exemption to small businesses based on square footage, regardless of the mode of reception, and then further expanded the exemption to allow businesses of any size to play licensed music if the number and location of loudspeakers was limited, if the establishment did not charge to hear the music transmitted, and if the broadcast was not transmitted beyond that establishment.

This blew a hole in music licensing in the U.S., but there was not much that U.S. artists could do about it. The Irish Music Rights Organization (IMRO), the collective society representing Irish musicians, convinced the EU to bring a

20 https://www.wto.org/english/tratop_e/dispu_e/cases_e/ds160_e.htm; accessed, December 19, 2021.

dispute settlement case against the United States under the TRIPS rules, rules that the U.S. had strongly advocated for at the time of the creation of the WTO. A WTO dispute panel found the U.S. in violation of its TRIPS commitments. The U.S. accepted the panel's ruling and agreed to try to bring its legal regime into compliance, but the U.S. administration was unable to get Congress to agree. It was estimated that the amount of revenue lost to IMRO was $1.1 million per year. The U.S. reached an agreement with the EU to pay $3.3 million for the first three years, pending further resolution. At the end of the three-year period, however, Congress was no closer to passing a law to remedy the situation. That is the situation that persists to this day. Each time the EU brings up the issue at the WTO, the U.S. delegation replies, in effect, that they are working on it. The response that the U.S. has repeated over 180 times over the years is, "The U.S. Administration will work closely with the U.S. Congress and will continue to confer with the European Union in order to reach a mutually satisfactory resolution of this matter."[21] All this just goes to prove that in a rules-based system, if you are big enough, you can get away with just about anything.

This also underscores that, despite international treaties, it is national legislatures that have final say over copyright law. The British Parliament enacted the Statute of Anne. The U.S. Congress passed the 1790 Copyright Act based on

21 https://docs.wto.org/dol2fe/Pages/SS/directdoc.aspx?filename=q:/WT/DS/160-24A197.pdf&Open=True; accessed December 19, 2021.

the U.S. Constitution. The Canadian Parliament legislated its first Copyright Act in 1868 in the aftermath of Confederation and has amended it several times since. Copyright has adapted with technology, but the underlying principles remain the same: to give authors the exclusive right to exploit their works for a limited time, subject to certain exceptions, in order to benefit the broader public by providing the incentive for the creation of original works. This is in parallel with the continental tradition of rights that derive from the concept of natural property, allowing authors to protect the integrity of their creations.

SUMMARY

Copyright has evolved over several hundred years, dating back to the 1710 Statute of Anne and before. It grew originally out of the desire of printers to protect their monopolies and has developed over the years to encompass a wide range of creative activities. Initially, copyright was restricted to national jurisdictions, which encouraged publishers in other countries to take advantage of the legal limitations of copyright enforcement to profit from printing unauthorized and unlicensed editions. To combat this problem, some countries negotiated bilateral copyright treaties, but these proved inadequate. In 1886, the Berne Convention, the first international copyright treaty, was signed between eight states. Since then, the convention has been expanded in both geographic coverage (to the point where there are now 181 members) and inclusion of new forms of communication. To supplement Berne, other international conventions covering specific kinds of communication rights have been concluded over the past few decades, culminating in the inclusion of copyright rules in the World Trade Organization through the TRIPS agreement, bringing copyright disputes under the WTO's dispute settlement process. Since the conclusion of TRIPS, two internet-related copyright treaties have been concluded.

CHAPTER 3

The Other Side of Copyright: Limitations and Exceptions

SO FAR, WE have discussed the bundle of rights that constitute copyright, the origin of these rights, and how they have developed over the past three and a half centuries. There is another important side to copyright — what it does *not* cover, and the exceptions built into it. To be eligible for copyright protection, a work must be original, must involve the expression of an idea (rather than the idea itself), and must be recorded in some form of concrete medium, often referred to as fixation.

ORIGINALITY

The question of originality is not straightforward. How much originality is required for a work to qualify for copyright protection? For a work to be original, it does not have to be the novel of the year, but it must be the independent work of the author and display, in American jurisprudence, a "modicum of creativity."[1] The Canadian definition relies on the exercise of "skill and judgment."[2], the criteria used to determine originality. A child's finger painting can be original if it uses some skill and judgment. Clearly the determination can be very subjective. The term "originality" is not defined in Berne, nor in national legislation. Given the virtual impossibility of defining precisely what it means, the question has been dealt with by the courts based on specific cases. For example, should a database that requires substantial time and investment to create, but that may not have many or any elements of originality, be protected? The white pages of the telephone book (remember them?) are the most obvious example. The U.S. Supreme Court, in what is considered a landmark ruling,[3] found that the selection and arrangement of pages in a typical phone book is not sufficiently creative to be protected by copyright. Some databases and compilations, however, have been protected where creative choices were made in the selection and layout of content. The so-called "sweat of the brow" principle is not enough to warrant

1 U.S. Copyright Office, Compendium, Copyright Authorship: What Can be Registered, Section 308.2; https://www.copyright.gov/comp3/chap300 /ch300-copyrightable-authorship.pdf; accessed February 2, 2022.

2 Canadian Intellectual Property Office, Copyright Basics, https://www .ic.gc.ca/eic/site/cipointernet-internetopic.nsf/eng/wr04784.html#wb-cont; accessed February 2, 2022.

3 Feist Publications Inc, v Rural Telephone Service Co, 499 US 340 (1991); https://supreme.justia.com/cases/federal/us/499/340/; accessed January 7, 2022.

protection. Thus, the operative criterion for protection is whether the author has made a creative choice when preparing the material.[4]

THE IDEA/EXPRESSION DICHOTOMY

One could argue that today there are no ideas left under the sun that are truly original. All ideas and knowledge are built on those that preceded them. But copyright is not about ideas. It concerns the expression of ideas. You and I can both have a similar idea but express it differently. Our idea could be a plot for a play, the composition of a painting, or a series of dance moves. Even though our ideas might be similar, each of us would express that idea in our own way. This is known as the idea/expression dichotomy. Expressions of ideas can be copyrighted; ideas cannot. Here is an example.

Yann Martel's Booker Prize–winning novel (and later award-winning film) *Life of Pi* was based on the premise of a boy sharing a boat with a tiger on a trans-Pacific voyage. Martel was accused by Brazilian author Moacyr Scliar of stealing this idea from his novel *Max and the Cats*. In Scliar's novel, written twenty years previously, a Brazilian boy and a panther cross the Atlantic together in a boat. Scliar accused Martel of plagiarism, and worse, and his publisher contemplated legal action for copyright

---

4 For an extensive discussion of the role of originality in copyright see Daniel J. Gervais, *(Re)structuring Copyright*, Cheltenham UK and Northampton, MA, Elgar, 2019, pp. 94–119.

infringement. Martel freely admitted he had been inspired to adopt the "boy and animal in boat" concept by reading a review of Scliar's work but said he hadn't read the novel itself. The case didn't go to court. Scliar dropped the issue after a conversation with Martel, but it is doubtful that Scliar or his publisher would have had much of a legal leg to stand on. People sharing boats with animals is an idea. Scliar's novel was an expression of that idea, but so was Martel's.

A recent case[5] documenting how an idea cannot be protected by copyright involved Montreal visual artist Claude Bouchard, who sued UNICEF and Ikea for appropriating her concept of making soft toys based on original drawings by children. Bouchard had originally sold her plush toys in a UNICEF outlet in Montreal. Ikea held a drawing competition for children and then produced toys based on the winning designs, donating some of the profits to UNICEF. Bouchard first tried to sue UNICEF for copying her toys, but the suit was dismissed because of UNICEF's protected status as an agency of the United Nations carrying out its mandate. Bouchard then sued Ikea, alleging that the toys infringed the following elements of her work:

5 Bouchard c. Ikea Canada, 2021 QCCS 1376 (CanLII), Cour Supérieure, Quebec, January 28, 2021; https://www.canlii.org/fr/qc/qccs/doc/2021 /2021qccs1376/2021qccs1376.html; accessed December 31, 2021. This account is based on the article by Gabrielle Mathieu and Alain Y. Dussault, "Can an Idea, Style or Method Be Protected Under the Copyright Act?" Lavery Lawyers, December 15, 2021; https://www.lavery.ca/en /publications/our-publications/4289-can-an-idea-style-or-method-be -protected-under-the-copyright-act-.html; accessed December 31, 2021.

- Round eyes cut from non-fraying fabrics and sewn around the edges;
- Thinly cut linear mouths sewn into non-fraying fabrics;
- Polyester fibre stuffing;
- The toy is proportionate to the size of children's hands;
- Soft toy faithful to the child's drawing;
- Child's name and age on the tag;
- Everything is solid (head, body, legs, and tail), in the same plane and stuffed;
- Use of textiles, plush, and the original colours of the drawings

The court determined that any copying by Ikea was not substantive because its toys were based on totally different designs executed by different children. But the main conclusion of the court was that Bouchard was trying to lay claim to copyright for an "idea, concept, style or method." There are only so many ways to make children's plush toys, and many of the conditions are governed by safety standards. Whereas she had argued that Ikea had copied her work in a broad sense, rather than individual works, the court dismissed her claim because the Copyright Act does not protect a body of work but rather each individual work.

THE MERGER DOCTRINE AND *SCÈNES À FAIRE*

Sometimes it is difficult to separate an idea from its expression. When these become conflated, it is referred to as merging or the merger doctrine. In effect, under this doctrine the expression of the idea has merged with the idea itself. In such cases, copyright does not apply because copyrighting the expression would result in constraining the free use of the idea. A good example is the so-called jewelled bee case. In this case, a jewelled pin in the shape of a bee was the subject of litigation. Would a similar jewel-encrusted pin in the shape of a bee created by another jeweller be an infringement of the copyright of the original jeweller? This was the question the court had to address in Herbert Rosenthal Jewelry Corp v Kalpakian.[6] The court decided, on the basis of the merger doctrine, that the idea of a jewelled bee could not be protected by copyright, although the defendants could not copy every aspect of the original piece of jewellery (which they had not done, arguing that they had derived the design by studying actual bees). Because the idea of a bee and its jewelled expression could not be separated, making a jewelled bee was not an infringement of copyright.

A similar concept to the merger doctrine applies in the area of writing, referred to as *scènes à faire*. This encompasses "elements of an original work that are so trite or

---

6 Herbert Rosenthal Jewelry Corp. v Kalpakian - 446 F.2d 738 (9th Cir. 1971); https://www.lexisnexis.com/community/casebrief/p/casebrief -herbert-rosenthal-jewelry-corp-v-kalpakian; accessed December 20, 2021

common that they are not captured by copyright."[7] There have been several well-known cases in the U.S. where the courts have ruled that common elements of a plot cannot be copyrighted. For example, two police dramas set in the Bronx both involving Irish cops, prostitutes, and drinking would not necessarily involve copyright infringement because you likely couldn't tell a police story in that setting without involving such characters and storylines. A recent case based on the same principles involved a suit against Disney by two screenwriters who accused the studio of lifting copyright-protected elements from their screenplay to produce *Pirates of the Caribbean*. The court dismissed the case,[8] pointing out that the similarities between the leading protagonists of both works were common characteristics of pirates: "cockiness, bravery, and drunkenness are generic, non-distinct characteristics which are not protectable."[9]

FIXATION

Most countries, including Canada[10] and the U.S., require that a work be fixed — that is, incorporated in a material

7 Duhaime's Law Dictionary; https://www.duhaime.org/Legal-Dictionary /Term/ScenesAFaire; accessed December 20, 2021.

8 Arthur Lee Alfred II et al. v The Walt Disney Company, et al. C.D. Cal; No. 18-8074 5/13/19; https://src.bna.com/IbC; accessed December 20, 2021.

9 Ibid. Page 9 at paragraphs 21–22.

10 Fixation is neither defined nor explicitly discussed in the Copyright Act as a general criterion for copyright protection but has been developed through court cases. Lesley Ellen Harris, *Canadian Copyright Law*, John Wiley & Sons, 2014, p. 26ff.

form that is more than fleeting.[11] If a work is not fixed in a concrete medium, it is generally not protected by copyright. Like so much in copyright, however, this seems straightforward but can have some interesting wrinkles. On a basic level, if someone told you orally about their idea of a plot for a book but did not write it down, it is not subject to copyright protection. If someone hummed an original tune but did not score it on paper, it is not protectable. If, however, they recorded what they told you or hummed, it could be.

According to the U.S. Copyright Office, fixation requires that a work be "fixed in any tangible medium of expression, now known or later developed, from which [it] can be perceived, reproduced, or otherwise communicated, either directly or indirectly with the aid of a machine or device."[12] In Canada, there is no specific requirement for fixation, although it is implicit.

The need for fixation raises some intriguing questions. For example, is a professionally sculpted sandcastle, like

11 The Berne Convention has a flexible fixation standard, permitting states to prescribe fixation in whatever manner they choose. Common law countries such as the U.S., the UK, Australia, and Canada maintain a fixation requirement, while civil law countries, including most European and Asian nations, do not. Some countries, such as Russia, Japan, and China, protect oral works. See Elizabeth White, "The Berne Convention's Flexible Fixation Requirement: A Problematic Provision for User-Generated Content," *Chicago Journal of International Law*, Volume 13, No. 2, January 1, 2013; https://chicagounbound.uchicago.edu/cgi/viewcontent .cgi?article=1385&context=cjil; accessed February 3, 2022.

12 U.S. Copyright Office, Compendium, Section 305; https://www .copyright.gov/comp3/chap300/ch300-copyrightable-authorship.pdf; accessed December 21, 2021.

those at Parksville, BC's annual sandcastle contest, subject to copyright? Is an original ice sculpture like those at Québec City's annual winter festival protectable? A sandcastle will normally be washed away by the incoming tide. In the case of Parksville, the castles are above the high-tide mark, but eventually they will be dissolved by rain, when the summer is over. Québec City's ice sculptures will last only until a thaw comes, but what about an ice sculpture crafted at a hotel as a centrepiece and kept in the hotel freezer? It would be fixed as long as the freezer worked, but perhaps not permanently. But permanence is not required for fixation.

How about a cake design on a cake that will eventually be eaten? A U.S. law firm looked at a real situation where the cake for Barack Obama's inauguration was copied by the Trump administration, which ordered an exact replica from a different bakery.[13] The question was whether the original cake designer could sue for copyright infringement. This article pointed out that for legal action to be taken on a copyright case in the U.S., the copyright must be registered with the U.S. Copyright Office (which it wasn't) and questioned whether baking a layer cake and decorating it with designs using the Great Seal of the United States was sufficiently original. We will never know because no case was brought. But the transitory nature of the cake did not seem to be an issue.

13   JD Supra; "A Tale of Two Cakes: Can Copyright Law Protect this Cake Design?", Cynthia Blake Sanders and Baker Donelson, January 23, 2017; https://www.jdsupra.com/legalnews/a-tale-of-two-cakes-can-copyright-law-49760/.

There is a simple solution to the dilemma of whether a work is fixed, and that is to take a photograph of the sandcastle or ice sculpture, thus capturing its design in a fixed medium. But a photo is owned by the photographer, not the owner of the object being photographed, so if you are making that definitive sandcastle and want to protect your design, take the photo yourself. However, a photograph may not be the only means to protect a transitory work by fixing it. In a recent case in the UK, while the end product — in that case a design embossed into a makeup powder palette — disappeared as soon as it was used and was thus transitory, the copyright on the design was upheld because the design itself was recorded.[14]

There are other limitations to copyright that go beyond originality, ideas versus expressions, and fixation.

MINIMAL USE

We have already noted in Chapter 1 that a substantial part of a work has to be used without permission for there to be an infringement, with substantiality dependent on more than just quantity. Conversely, if only a limited amount of a work is used, this could qualify as an exception. It is generally accepted that very limited uses such as short

14 Islestarr Holdings v Aldi Stores Ltd, June 17, 2019, at para 114; https://www.bailii.org/ew/cases/EWHC/Ch/2019/1473.html; accessed November 2, 2022; Jeremy Blum and Marc Linsner, "Using Copyright to stop copycats"; Islestarr Holdings v Aldi Stores Ltd, September 2, 2019; http://copyrightblog.kluweriplaw.com/2019/09/02/using-copyright-to-stop -copycats-islestarr-holdings-ltd-v-aldi-stores-ltd/; accessed November 2, 2022.

words or phrases would likely not constitute copyright infringement. Minimal use (or *de minimis*) is not defined in legislation but is certainly a consideration in determining if a work is protectable.

FACTS

Just as ideas cannot be copyrighted, neither can facts. This has led to considerable debate over whether news reporting can be protected by copyright. The Berne Convention expressly excludes "news of the day" from copyright protection. But what about a news report that was the result of extensive investigative journalism that produced a scoop for the media outlet concerned? Should other media be allowed to simply reproduce the report without permission? This issue has been debated for many years.

Back in the nineteenth century, it was accepted practice for newspapers to cut and paste copy from rival publications. In the early days of radio, announcers often simply read newspaper headlines over the air. This led to protracted litigation in several countries over what aspects of news gathering could be protected, and the debate continues to this day.

While it is by now well established that publishers, broadcasters, and journalists can exercise copyright over news reports that involve creative expression, the separation of facts from expression is not always straightforward. What about a news headline? Does it just convey the facts, or is it, as Agence France Presse (AFP) contended in its 2005 suit against Google,[15] a creative expression capturing qualitatively the most important aspects of a story, painstakingly created? (The case was settled out of court, leading to a licensing agreement for AFP content.) If a piece of content is protected by copyright, does reproduction of a snippet constitute fair use/fair dealing, or does the publication of the snippet reveal the essence of the content and undermine the publisher's economic rights? This issue is at the root of disputes between online news aggregators such as Google News and social media platforms like Facebook and news publishers over reproduction of snippets and headlines by the online platforms without licensing or payment. This is covered in more detail in Chapter 6.

HUMAN CREATION

It may seem obvious that for a work to be protected by copyright it must be created by a human, but copyright has many wrinkles. For example, could a copyrighted work be created by a machine, such as music composed by or art created by an algorithm? If so, who owns the copyright? This is a current issue that will be explored in Chapter 7.

A related question is whether a work created by an animal could be copyrighted. If an infinite number of monkeys on an infinite number of typewriters worked long

15 Reuters, Eric Auchard, April 7, 2007; "AFP, Google News settle lawsuit over Google News"; https://www.reuters.com/article/us-google -afp-idUSN0728115420070407; accessed December 21, 2021.

enough, they could produce the works of Shakespeare. Or that at least is how the infinite monkey theorem credited to noted French mathematician Emile Borel (who sadly is more remembered for his monkey example than his other considerable contributions to the science of mathematics) was used to illustrate his thoughts on probability in 1913. The works of Shakespeare are not subject to copyright protection since they have long been in the public domain,[16] but what if, instead of the works of Shakespeare, those simian creators produced an original work? Would that work be protected by copyright, and if so, who would own it? Would it be the owner of the typewriter(s) who conceived of and organized the event and thus made the outcome possible, and who then sifted through the disorganized mass of typed papers to select material to compile an intelligible work from the random keying of the band of monkeys? Would it be the monkeys? Or would it perhaps be no one? Suppose an infinite number of monkeys — or even a few monkeys, or even one monkey — could produce another form of art, like a painting or a photograph? Who would own the copyright? This question is at the heart of the famous (or infamous) monkey selfie case and the controversy surrounding noted wildlife photographer David Slater.[17]

---

16 The concept of public domain is explained in more detail below.

17 "The Monkey Selfie Case: Applying the Common Sense Test," Hugh-StephensBlog, June 27, 2016; https://hughstephensblog.net/2016/06/27/the-monkey-selfie-case-applying-the-common-sense-test/; accessed December 21, 2021.

On a trip to Sulawesi, Indonesia, in 2011 to photograph primates, Slater noticed the interest of a band of macaques in his photographic equipment. Initially, they took his camera and ran off with it. One monkey even pressed the shutter of the stolen camera, perhaps by mistake or by learning from watching Slater. However, these photographs were of the ground or too blurred to be useful. But this gave Slater an idea. He experimented with various setups, configured the camera's settings, and mounted it on a tripod, which he held while members of the band groomed him. The macaques remained fascinated and manipulated the camera, in the process releasing the shutter again. Several were of sufficient quality to be worthy of reproduction, particularly one photo where a particular macaque (whom someone named "Naruto") was fascinated with his (or her) reflection in the lens. Naruto mugged for the camera and managed to trigger the device. One of the photos was reminiscent of a human posing for a selfie, with a silly smile.

Slater developed the photo and licensed it through a photographic agency. The story went viral when it was picked up by the news media as the "monkey selfie story." Slater benefited from the publicity and managed to earn a couple of thousand pounds sterling from licensing the photo. The story then morphed into a copyright issue when Wikipedia decided that it would put up the macaque photo for public use on Wikimedia Commons on the basis that Slater did not own the copyright since the monkey, not he, had actually taken the photograph. An inconclusive exchange followed, with Slater requesting that Wikipedia take the photo down, Wikipedia refusing, threats of a lawsuit, etc. Slater estimated that he lost at least £10,000 in licensing fees as a result of Wikipedia's position.

As if that weren't enough monkey business, the animal rights group People for the Ethical Treatment of Animals (PETA), in what was a brilliant publicity stunt, upped the ante by bringing suit in California alleging that the copyright was actually owned by Naruto the macaque on the basis that it was he (or she) who had actually triggered the camera's shutter. This also went viral, under the catchy byline "monkey see, monkey sue," a phrase coined by Slater's lawyers in their filing to have the case dismissed. That, in the end, was what happened, with Judge William Orrick ruling that a non-human was not capable of owning copyright under current U.S. law.[18] Among the references cited was a clarification of conditions of copyright registration issued by the U.S. Copyright Office stating that animals could not register copyrights, giving as specific examples a photograph taken by a monkey or a mural painted by an elephant. PETA appealed the dismissal of the case, and,

18   "Naruto, a Crested Macaque, by and through his Next Friends, People for the Ethical Treatment of Animals, and Antje Engelhardt, Ph.d v. David John Slater, an individual, Blurb Inc, a Delaware Company and Wildlife Personalities Ltd, a United Kingdom Private Company", Case 3:15-cv-04324-WHO; United States District Court, Northern District of California; https://www.documentcloud.org/documents/2678125-Motion-to-Dismiss-Naruto-Case; accessed December 21, 2021.

in frustration, Slater agreed to a settlement whereby he agreed to donate 25 percent of the proceeds from the photograph to macaque welfare projects in Indonesia.[19]

What was never determined was whether Slater actually owned the copyright in the photograph. Applying the common-sense test, it clearly belonged to him. Would the photo have been taken without his equipment, efforts, and staging? Would the photo have been selected, developed, printed, and distributed without his efforts? Did Slater engage in a creative act in bringing about the production of the photo? In photography, is the mere act of pushing the shutter the act of creation, or is it the staging, technical settings, composition, selection, etc. that is the true test of creativity? These are all relevant questions.

PUBLIC DOMAIN

One thing is clear. A work created exclusively by an animal is in the public domain and therefore is free to use without recourse to a copyright holder. Public domain works are free for anyone to use without permission because either copyright does not apply to them or their term of copyright protection has expired. Mozart's works are in the public domain, as are Shakespeare's. A recent recording of a Mozart work, however, is not free to use, as copyright

19 National Public Radio, Jason Slotkin, September 12, 2017, "'Monkey Selfie' Lawsuit Ends With Settlement Between PETA, Photographer," https://www.npr.org/sections/thetwo-way/2017/09/12/550417823/-animal -rights-advocates-photographer-compromise-over-ownership-of-monkey -selfie; accessed December 21, 2021.

will exist in the performance. Likewise, a recent annotated edition of Shakespeare's works is likely protected by copyright because of the editorial notes.

In the United States, works produced by the U.S. federal government are in the public domain. In contrast, in Canada, government works and works produced by agencies under government control fall under Crown copyright, with copyright protection lasting for fifty years (as of the time of writing) from the date of publication.

Under *droit d'auteur*, copyright is considered a natural law property right. This has led to arguments that copyright duration should not be limited any more than other property rights are. Under an economic rights theory, the monopoly conferred by copyright should be limited both in time and application in order to provide a balance between authors' and users' rights.

USER EXCEPTIONS

In addition to the time limit on copyright, there are user exceptions allowing unlicensed use in specified ways and for specified purposes. If a use falls within the listed exceptions (in the United States, the list is illustrative), the user may be permitted to use copyrighted material without authorization, subject to certain conditions. These unlicensed uses are known as fair dealing in Canada, the UK, and many countries where copyright laws are based on British legislation. In the United States, the exceptions are referred to as fair use, a more open-ended doctrine.

In Canada, fair dealing, which is not actually defined in legislation, is based on the 1921 Copyright Act, which in turn was based on the 1911 UK statute that established the concept of fair dealing within British law. The 1911 UK act is the basis for fair dealing legislation in most Commonwealth countries, such as Canada, Australia, New Zealand, South Africa, India, and some others. Fair dealing exceptions have evolved over the years in response to changing needs and technology and are no longer identical in all Commonwealth jurisdictions. In most countries, there is a periodic review and update as needed.

Each country's list varies slightly, but generally exceptions are allowed for research, private study, parody, satire, criticism, review, and news reporting. Some of these exceptions require citation of the original source. In addition to these longstanding exceptions, newer ones have been added in some countries to include education and data mining. Canada is one of the first countries to include a broad exception for education, a decision that has led to considerable controversy, several court cases, and significant damage to the Canadian publishing industry. The education exception can be invoked by anyone, not just educational institutions. I will discuss this in more detail in Chapter 6. Even if a use falls within the definition of a fair dealing exception, it is subject to other tests such as the purpose, character, amount, alternatives, nature, and effect of the use.

Canada also provides an exception for user-generated

content if not done for commercial purposes, as well as exceptions such as making a private copy of a sound recording, shifting the format of a legally acquired recording, recording a broadcast or performance for later viewing (time shifting), making backup copies of content and computer programs, and reproducing a computer work for encryption research.[20] There are also various exceptions for designated educational institutions. They may make unlicensed copies of a work in order to display it for instructional purposes, for tests and exams, and for distance learning (provided the original works were legitimately obtained), and they may show films and programs and perform musical works for educational purposes if the audience is composed primarily of students.

The courts in Canada have played a role in defining what uses are fair. The Supreme Court of Canada has stated that "research" must be given a "large and liberal interpretation" and that "private study" includes study in a classroom.[21]

In the United States, the fair use doctrine developed over many years through legal interpretations delivered by courts, although it was finally codified in the U.S. Copyright Act in 1976. Some have argued that fair use is more flexible than fair dealing, although it is also more unpredictable and tends to lead to more litigation. While fair use

20 Harris, *Canadian Copyright Law*, Wiley, 2014, pp. 168–176.

21 Harris, p. 167.

in the U.S. is subject to four specified fair use factors,[22] its interpretation depends on each case's particular circumstances and the decisions of individual courts. Different circuits of the U.S. federal courts have at times delivered conflicting interpretations of what constitutes fair use.

Because of the uncertainty as to whether a use in the U.S. falls within the definition of fair use, the U.S. Copyright Office has produced a Fair Use Index[23] to guide users. As the index notes, "Courts evaluate fair use claims on a case-by-case basis, and the outcome of any given case depends on a fact-specific inquiry. This means that there is no formula to ensure that a predetermined percentage or amount of a work — or specific number of words, lines, pages, copies — may be used without permission." The complexity of the index is a good reason why the relative certainty of fair dealing has proven attractive to many jurisdictions. Although the term "fair use" is often used colloquially in Canada to mean an unlicensed use that may be allowed by law, the U.S. fair use doctrine and its legal precedents have no application outside the United States.

---

22 These factors are (1) Purpose and character of the use, including whether the use is of a commercial nature or is for nonprofit educational purposes; (2) Nature of the copyrighted work; (3) Amount and substantiality of the portion used in relation to the copyrighted work as a whole; and (4) Effect of the use upon the potential market for or value of the copyrighted work.

23 U.S. Copyright Office Fair Use Index; https://www.copyright.gov /fair-use/; accessed December 21, 2021.

CREATIVE COMMONS LICENCES

As we have seen, if a work is in the public domain, either because copyright protection has expired or due to lack of copyright coverage for various reasons such as non-substantial use or lack of originality of the work, there is no requirement to obtain permission for use, to acquire a licence authorizing use, or to pay for use. In addition, provided the use falls within fair use or fair dealing or other specified exceptions, there is no need for recourse to the copyright holder.

There is, however, one additional category of work where payment of royalties is not required, although a licence must still be obtained. These are works that have been placed under the Creative Commons (CC) system by their authors. Creative Commons[24] is a not-for-profit U.S. society established in 2001 to provide authors with the means to license use of their content without requiring payment. Authors cannot renounce copyright; it is conferred automatically upon the creation of a qualifying work. But they can choose to not exercise their prerogative to collect payment for certain uses of their work — in other words, not to exercise some or all of their economic rights.

Creative Commons offers a simple means for them to do so, by opting into the system and offering users a CC licence. CC licences allow licensees to copy, distribute, display, or perform the work, make a digital performance, or shift it to another format. A CC licence endures for

24 See https://creativecommons.org/; accessed December 23, 2021.

the same period as copyright over a work, applies globally, and is not revocable or exclusive. It may be subject to limitations such as no commercial use, no creation of derivative works, or a requirement to share (through a CC licence) any subsequent works created with the material. Attribution (recognition) of the original author is required. Users do not need to apply for a CC licence per se; rather, they can use the materials in accordance with the licence conditions specified, but they must cite the author and the type of CC licence they are using. Using the licence in effect means agreeing to the terms established by Creative Commons.

Why, you might ask, would authors renounce their economic rights? Many copyright holders are determined to protect their economic interests. After all, for many, it is their sole or primary livelihood. They go to great lengths to protect their copyright interests (see Chapter 4). But for some authors, economic return is not their primary consideration. Many are academics who are paid to undertake and publish research. You might say that it is part of their day job. Many of these academics are also in the forefront of opposition to strong copyright laws from a philosophical perspective, arguing that copyright law gets in the way of the free sharing of knowledge.[25] It is easy to argue for free information if your work is subsidized in some other way.

25 "The Future of Creative Commons," 2013, p. 4; https://wiki
.creativecommons.org/images/c/ce/Future-of-creative-commons.pdf;
accessed December 22, 2021.

SUMMARY

This chapter has summarized the situations where copyright does not apply or where it is limited by specified exceptions. It has also given examples of where free, voluntary licences may be granted. Exceptions to copyright have evolved over time, as technology has changed, and will no doubt continue to do so.

CHAPTER 4

Copyright Piracy:
Its Manifestations and Motivations

TODAY, DESPITE THE many ways in which consumers can use content created by others without permission, licensing, or payment, either because the content is in the public domain or is accessible through legal exceptions to copyright protection, there is still a significant percentage of the public that chooses to avoid paying for the copyrighted content they consume. This is facilitated by infringing websites and online services that are often based outside the boundaries of the jurisdictions in which most of the consumers reside. These are the infamous offshore pirate websites and streaming services that are so ubiquitous, and so difficult to shut down.

WHAT IS CONTENT PIRACY?
Both piracy and counterfeiting have been around for a long time. The simple distinction between the two is that in counterfeiting, someone is trying to pass off a fake as the

real thing. That bargain Gucci purse is not really a Gucci at all. Perhaps the branded brake linings that are being installed in your car are also not the real deal. In the case of piracy, the product is real, but the use of that content is unauthorized and infringing. The use of the term "piracy" to describe theft of intellectual property rights goes back to the seventeenth century, even before the enactment of the Statute of Anne, when London booksellers used the term to describe competitors who reprinted their works without authorization.[1]

The primary definition of piracy, of course, has to do with seaborne corsairs plundering ships and coastal towns, often brutally. Maritime piracy was a major scourge from the seventeenth through nineteenth centuries, and pirates were feared and detested. The public image of pirates began to change with the publication of Robert Louis Stevenson's *Treasure Island* and the complex character of Long John Silver, immortalized in the 1951 Disney film of the same name starring Robert Newton. (Arrgh, matey.) More recently, Captain Jack Sparrow of the *Pirates of the Caribbean* franchise has made being a pirate even more respectable with his cunning, swashbuckling character. Through these characterizations, piracy has taken on an almost Robin Hood–like aspect. A good example of the brand image of piracy is the proud adoption of the name The Pirate Bay by the notorious Swedish content piracy site.

The term "piracy" has been widely applied both to the

---

1 Adrian Johns, *Piracy: The Intellectual Property Wars from Gutenberg to Gates*, Chicago and London, University of Chicago Press, 2009, pp. 17–40.

illegal copying of works as well as where unauthorized reproduction was legal but perhaps unethical. This was particularly true in the nineteenth century, when copyright laws were restricted to national application. Thus, Charles Dickens famously criticized "Yankee pirates" for stealing his work through legal but unauthorized editions printed in the U.S., while Mark Twain took aim at "Canadian thieves" for printing unauthorized editions of *The Adventures of Tom Sawyer*.[2] Twain is reported to have said, "I can't trust any more Canadians after my late experience. I suppose they are all born pirates."[3] Piracy was not just

2   Eli MacLaren, *Dominion and Agency: Copyright and the Structuring of the Canadian Book Trade, 1867–1918*, Toronto, University of Toronto Press, 2011, pp. 81–83. The reasons for Canadian piracy are complex and relate to Canada's subordinate position as a colony up to 1867 and a less than fully sovereign dominion after that date, along with its proximity to the United States. Canada tried unsuccessfully to pass copyright legislation on several occasions in the nineteenth century, only to have the legislation blocked by the Governor General on the advice of the British government, which was responding to pressures from the British book trade to protect their interests in the Canadian market. Unsuccessful in obtaining the rights to publish British works in Canada, some Canadian printers, notably the Belford Brothers, resorted to printing U.S. works (which was legally done in Canada at that time) just as U.S. printers freely reproduced British works. See MacLaren and Meera Nair, "The Geopolitics of Nineteenth-Century Canadian Copyright, as seen by some British Authors," *Papers of the Bibliographical Society of Canada*, Vol. 55, No. 2, 2017; https://jps.library. utoronto.ca/index.php/bsc/article/view/32287; accessed January 5. 2022.

3   Henry Nash Smith and William Gibson, eds, *Mark Twain-Howell's Letters*, I, pp. 166–167, Cambridge, MA, Harvard University Press, 1960, cited in "Mark Twain and His Canadian Publishers: A Second Look," nd, https://jps.library.utoronto.ca/index.php/bsc/article/view/16703/13685; accessed December 24, 2021.

restricted to foreigners. Dickens' famous work *A Christmas Carol* was pirated in England and reproduced in a condensed and slightly rewritten two-penny version by Parley's Illuminated Library. Dickens sued for copyright infringement and won, but the pirate publisher promptly declared bankruptcy, leaving Dickens to pay the court costs.[4]

The term "piracy" as a description for copyright infringement came into popular use once again with the advent of ubiquitous and cheap recording devices for music and audiovisual content. So-called bootleg (note once again the piracy analogy, bootleg products having originally been smuggled in the boots of pirates) copies of recordings were widely distributed in flea markets and similar places in the form of cassettes, VHS tapes, and, later, compact discs and DVDs. The association of copyright theft with piracy today is unfortunate given the romantic view of pirates propagated by Hollywood, leading to downplaying the seriousness of the offence. Copyright piracy is theft of intellectual property, although unlike physical theft, the author has not lost possession of the work. It is the rights that have been stolen.

With the arrival of the digital age, the problem of pirated content became more challenging for the music and film industries because with digital technology, each reproduction is perfect. Earlier reproduction techniques

---

4 Matthew Wills, "Pirating Charles Dickens' *A Christmas Carol*, in the 1840s", JSTOR *Daily*, December 26, 2019; https://daily.jstor.org/pirating-charles-dickens-a-christmas-carol-in-the-1840s/; accessed December 27, 2021.

had resulted in degraded quality the more copies that were reproduced. Sometimes pirated versions of films were shot in cinemas with poor recording quality and ambient background noise, giving a quality advantage to legitimate copies. The digital era not only allowed pirate producers to replicate perfect copies once they got their hands on a clean copy, it provided global and relatively anonymous distribution channels through the internet.

BOOK PIRACY

The question of protecting authorship and by extension publication rights was largely resolved through establishment of the Berne Convention in 1886, along with subsequent amendments, although there were always some countries that remained outside the internationally agreed rules. One of these was the Republic of China, which by 1949 had decamped to Taiwan. Since China had not acceded to Berne, Taiwan became a hotbed of book piracy. In fact, it was the epicentre of a thriving trade in pirated works, ranging from the bestsellers of the day to medical and other expensive textbooks to the Encyclopedia Britannica. At Tan Chiang Book Company on Chungking Road South in Taipei, full twenty-four-volume sets of the Encyclopedia Britannica retailed in those days for between $40 and $75, whereas the same sets would have cost $400 to $550 back in the U.S., depending on the quality of the binding. As reported in an article in the November 15, 1963, edition of *Life* Magazine written by Charles

Elliott, "Taiwan's Bestselling Pirates,"[5] the technique was simple. A Taiwan bookseller/publisher would have a friend purchase a copy of a newly released book in the U.S. or elsewhere and send it to him via airmail. Once received, it was disassembled, photocopied page by page, and then reproduced on an offset press, including, reportedly, a new German-built press purchased with U.S. government development assistance funds!

At that time the Kuomintang (KMT) regime on Taiwan was still recognized by most of the world as the legitimate government of China, even though it had retreated from the mainland in 1949 to what was then known as Formosa. But even though the KMT regime represented China at the United Nations and in most of the world's capitals, China was not a signatory to any of the international copyright conventions. Thus, it was perfectly legal under Chinese law to appropriate copyrighted material from abroad and reproduce it without payment to the author (much as U.S. publishers did with the works of Charles Dickens). Only by obtaining a Chinese copyright registration, which was notoriously difficult to do, could a work be protected in Taiwan (eventually, the Encyclopedia Britannica did just that). Not only were pirated western works openly available on the streets of Taipei in book emporiums such as Tan Chiang, enterprising students and others in the U.S.

5   Charles Elliott, "Chinese Book Pirates: U.S. Slows Down a Taiwan Publishing Racket. Special Report by Charles Elliott," *Life* Magazine, November 15, 1963; https://www.originallifemagazines.com/product /life-magazine-november-15-1963/; accessed December 24, 2021.

regularly made it a practice to procure their textbooks from Taiwan at a fraction of the American price, opening up a thriving grey market. This was well before the Internet had been conceived of, but catalogues mailed from Taiwan ensured that the wares were advertised in the U.S. within knowledgeable circles.

Publishers were not amused. Representations were made to the U.S. government, which was both Taiwan's security guarantor as well as its chief source of development assistance funds, to do something. By the early 1960s, the U.S. started to lean on the KMT government of Chiang Kai-shek to stop undermining the U.S. book market by forcing them to clamp down on book exports, even if the pirate publishers were allowed to remain in business in Taiwan. This was long before the U.S. Congress had developed any formalized process to bring pressure on foreign countries for permitting theft of U.S. intellectual property. The word was simply passed that this had to stop, and the "ingenious band of rascals," as Elliott described the Taiwanese book pirates, had to clip their wings.

MUSIC PIRACY: NAPSTER AND GROKSTER

If "piracy" is an abused term and a way of glossing over the reality of theft of an author's intellectual property rights, the term "file sharing" is an equal misnomer. It originated through the development of peer-to-peer (P2P) protocols on the internet. P2P networks harness the collective power of individual users, thereby avoiding the need for central servers or hosts. In the late 1990s, P2P technology was used by the Silicon Valley start-up Napster to create the world's first MP3 digital file sharing service; once the Napster software was downloaded by individual users, music files could be transmitted or shared among members of the network. Within weeks of its founding, Napster had millions of users. It was billed as an online library, except that no one was borrowing. They were accessing MP3 music files on the computers of other Napster users, downloading the files to their own computers, and burning CDs. It was free music, or at least that is how many users regarded it. Except that the music being offered up for free downloads by users was copyrighted, with the sharing being a violation of the terms of licensing prohibiting unauthorized reproduction that applied when the original music was sold.

Musicians and the recording industry were not amused as sales of CDs began to plummet. But who was responsible? Napster took the position that all it was doing was providing software. While the software could be used to distribute pirated music, it also had some legitimate uses such as sampling and the circulation of works in the public domain. Although Napster's servers played a role in relaying search requests from users, from Napster's perspective, it was either the uploaders who made the content available or the downloaders who took the music who were doing the pirating. Musicians were urged to accept the new technology as free advertising and instead earn a living through touring. Some did; most didn't. The initial response of the music industry was to bring suit against Napster. The seminal case was A&M Records v Napster in October 2000.[6] The U.S. Court of Appeals upheld a California court decision that had rejected Napster's arguments of fair use and found Napster liable for contributory and vicarious copyright infringement.[7]

Napster was forced out of business but was soon replaced by the next generation of file sharing services, such as Grokster, Kazaa, and others. Grokster differed from Napster in that it avoided maintaining any central register of files and was a pure P2P application; it also targeted former Napster users, and most of the traffic on its network was infringing. In 2005, in the legal case of MGM v Grokster,[8] the U.S. Supreme Court, on appeal, found Grokster liable for inducing copyright infringement of music and movies. Grokster closed down. In the meantime, the Recording Industry Association of America had launched a series of lawsuits against individual downloaders. Many cases were settled out of court by those accused, but in some instances, downloaders were fined substantial amounts (in

6 https://www.copyright.gov/fair-use/summaries/a&mrecords-napster -9thcir2001.pdf; accessed December 28, 2021.

7 Contributory and vicarious liability are both forms of secondary liability, but in the case of vicarious liability, direct knowledge of illegal behaviour is not required. The court found that Napster had direct knowledge that its service was being used for infringing purposes.

8 Metro-Goldwyn-Mayer Studios Inc v Grokster, Ltd, 545 U.S. (2005), https://www.copyright.gov/docs/mgm/; accessed December 28, 2021.

the thousands of dollars). In a few other cases, there was uncertainty as to who had done the actual downloading on an individual computer, leading to the inevitable headlines of grandmothers sued for downloading music, when poor granny did not even know how to turn on the computer.

Suing your potential customers is not a sustainable business model, however, and in the end the music industry was rescued by new technology and new music offerings, such as the iPod and Apple's online music store, since replicated by others. The ability to purchase music by track at low prices, combined with the threat of legal action for illegal downloading, eventually turned things around for music creators and their labels. Most P2P file sharers were aware that what they were doing was a violation of copyright law. They either didn't care, subscribing to the theory that whatever was on the internet should be free (ignoring the cost and effort of creation), or thought they wouldn't get caught, at least until the lawsuits started. In the end, the stick-and-carrot approach to protecting the livelihood of musicians, songwriters, performers, recording engineers, and all the others who contribute to the making of music seems to have worked, but it was a challenging period.

AUDIOVISUAL CONTENT AND BROADCASTING

The category of audiovisual works includes movies, TV series, documentaries, and music videos, among others. In many cases, especially in the case of movies or television series, a large part of the value of a property derives from timeliness. The period of maximum demand for a new film or an updated season of a television series is immediately after it is released. That is why movie studios spend heavily to promote a new release and why cable platforms bid to acquire newly released must-have content. A premature release of a pirated version can result in huge losses and undermine the entire value of blockbuster films and series. Sometimes the pirated version is copied from a "screener" — an advance copy of a film sent to critics or jury members for film festivals or screen awards — that has been inadvertently leaked. The pirate business model today is generally to distribute the content through a pirate website or streaming service, generating revenue either through advertising or, in some cases, subscriptions. These websites are usually registered in jurisdictions beyond the reach of domestic laws.

One effective means increasingly employed by countries around the world to fight this type of piracy is known as site blocking, perhaps more accurately described as disabling access to offshore pirate sites. Australia, the UK, and many European countries routinely use site blocking in the fight against content pirates. Initially, there was pushback from some telecommunications companies that provided internet connection services. These telecoms were concerned about incurring costs or antagonizing users, but in those countries where site blocking is now common practice, the process has been streamlined and costs have been kept low. Australia, which has implemented specific legislation governing site blocking, has established a nominal flat fee per blocking request. Some groups continue to argue that site blocking infringes individual freedoms and undermines net neutrality (the concept that a telecommunications carrier should not interfere with traffic on its networks or favour in-house content). But the internet freedom arguments do not stand up to close examination. Net neutrality applies to legal content; there is no requirement for carriers to facilitate illegal activity. As long as there is a transparent process to identify which sites are to be blocked, including an appeal process, it is hard to understand how freedom of expression is infringed beyond the reasonable limits already existent in law.

Some countries, like the UK and Australia, use court proceedings to reach blocking orders, while others have set up quasi-judicial regulatory agencies to manage the system. In Canada, while there have been proposals from copyright holders to establish an independent agency to implement a site-blocking system,[9] because of legal technicalities this

9   In early 2018, a coalition called Fair Play Canada was established to promote the creation of an Independent Piracy Review Agency that would be regulated by the Canadian Radio-television and Telecommunications Commission (CRTC). Fair Play Canada's members included several major unions, the public broadcaster CBC, five of the six largest national telecommunications providers, specialized TV providers, a major sports entertainment company, the country's largest film festival, several major cinema exhibition chains, independent cinema operators, independent film producers, and a combination of English-language, French-language, and ethnic media. After several months of hearings and consideration, the CRTC ruled that it did not have the jurisdiction under the Telecommunications Act to implement the coalition's proposed website blocking regime to

has not been implemented. In 2019, however, the Federal Court issued Canada's first site-blocking order against pirate operator GoldTV.[10] That order was upheld on appeal,[11] opening the way to more such orders in Canada. Several injunctions to require blocking of specific sites or specific content, like unauthorized broadcasts of live NHL games, have since been issued by the federal court. The U.S. remains one of the few developed countries that has not, to date, instituted any form of site blocking against online offshore pirate sites.

SPORTS BROADCAST PIRACY
Streaming rather than offering content for download is the most common form of content piracy today. Such streaming involves the unauthorized distribution of movies and television series, but also top-level sports programming. Sports has a very limited window in which to extract the value of its content; once the game is over, there is very little interest in it other than watching highlights. Sports leagues

address copyright piracy. CRTC Telecom Decision CRTC 2018-384; https://crtc.gc.ca/eng/archive/2018/2018-384.htm; accessed December 26, 2021.

10 Bell Media Inc. v GoldTV.Biz, 2019 FC 1432; https://www.canlii.org/en/ca/fct/doc/2019/2019fc1432/2019fc1432.html?searchUrlHash=AAAAAQAWY29weXJpZZh0IGluZnJpbmdlbWVudAAAAAB; accessed December 26, 2021.

11 The decision was not appealed by GoldTV, who were not represented and did not appear, but rather by one of the internet service providers, Teksavvy, that was required by the blocking order to take action to disable access by its customers to the offshore site maintained by GoldTV.biz.

license the broadcast rights to the games, with revenues used for everything from paying player salaries to investing in youth programs. In this sense, fans who cheat the league or the sport they love are only cheating themselves in the long run since the denial of revenues to legitimate providers that pay to license content only lowers their ability to pay in future, reducing revenues available to strengthen the game. Instead, revenue that could go toward developing the next generation of players is diverted to offshore pirate operators who skim the cream while contributing nothing to the sport.

One of the most prevalent forms of piracy today is the streaming of professional sports and other premium content through illicit streaming devices, boxes that can be configured to provide access to pirated content. Usually, these devices also have a legitimate purpose. They plug in to TV sets and serve to record, aggregate, and deliver online content to television viewers; however, through the addition of apps or by accessing offshore websites to download special software, users can have access to a wide variety of pirated content. Users even pay subscription fees to access cheaper pirated content in lieu of subscribing to licensed sports providers. Sellers of these boxes will often advertise them as gateways to "free TV." A 2017 study estimated the losses to legitimate content providers in the U.S. and Canada to be $840 million.[12]

---

12 "Spotlight: Subscription Television Piracy," Sandvine, Waterloo, ON, November 27, 2017; https://www.sandvine.com/hubfs/downloads/reports/

In the UK and some other countries, including Canada, the courts have allowed dynamic blocking orders as part of the suite of tools to combat sports piracy. This allows copyright holders to shift targets as the pirates duck and weave, constantly altering the online location of their illicit sports streams. They will shift website domain names and IP addresses, sometimes within a single game. The dynamic orders allow copyright holders to react quickly without having to go back to court for a new order for each change of address, often resulting in interruption of the pirated game stream in real time. There is nothing more frustrating to a soccer fan than to lose TV coverage just before the winning goal is scored. This technique has helped combat sports piracy, resulting in greater uptake of legitimate services where uninterrupted service can be guaranteed.

THE COST OF PIRACY

While piracy is a problem for all authors and copyright industries, in recent years it has primarily punished the music, film, and television industries, and the cost is large. It is estimated that at present, about 80 percent of piracy is attributable to streaming, costing the U.S. content industry almost $30 billion annually. The U.S. Chamber of Commerce estimated that it also costs the U.S. economy between 230,000 and 560,000 jobs and between $47.5 billion and $115.3 billion in reduced gross domestic product

internet-phenomena/sandvine-spotlight-subscription-television-piracy.pdf; accessed December 31, 2021.

(GDP) each year.[13] These are figures for the U.S. economy alone. On a global scale, the costs of piracy are much greater. An authoritative study by Frontier Economics in 2015 estimated the global value of digital piracy in movies, music, and software to be $213 billion.[14] That study forecast that this amount would increase to between $384 and $856 billion in five years, depending on assumptions as to whether the rate of piracy remains stable or grows with greater internet use. The estimated value is a composite of losses to legitimate industries and creators, costs to defend against intellectual property infringement, losses of government revenue, and the diversion of public and private resources from more productive ends into the illegal acquisition of intellectual property. These costs are a significant drag on the growth of knowledge-based economies and employment.

In Canada, overall estimates of piracy are hard to come by, but Bell Media has estimated that the financial impact of just television piracy on Canadian broadcasters and distributors is in the range of $500 million to $650 million per year, affecting thousands of jobs across the

13   David Blackburn, Jeffrey A. Eisenach and David Harrison, Jr., "Impacts of Digital Piracy on the U.S. Economy," Nera Economic Consulting and Global Innovation Policy Centre, June 2019; https://www.theglobalipcenter.com/wp-content/uploads/2019/06/Digital-Video-Piracy.pdf; accessed December 31, 2021.

14   Frontier Economics, "The Economic Impacts of Counterfeiting and Piracy," Frontier Economics, February 6, 2017; https://www.iccwbo.be/wp-content/uploads/2017/02/ICC-BASCAP-INTA-2016-report.pdf; accessed December 31, 2021.

industry.[15] Whatever the actual cost, and it can be calculated in different ways, the impact of piracy cuts across the creative ecosphere, affecting writers, producers, technicians, broadcasting enterprises, and legitimate retailers, not to mention tax revenues. The flip side of the economic losses are the economic contributions made by the cultural sector, almost all of which are protected by copyright. In Canada, cultural industries contributed $57.1 billion to the Canadian economy in 2019,[16] or just under 3 percent of GDP, sustaining 772,000 jobs. However, there was a decline of 6 percent in 2020 owing to the impact of the COVID-19 pandemic.[17]

If those figures sound impressive, the U.S. numbers are even more so. Core copyright industries in the U.S. contributed 7.41 percent of GDP, or a total value of $1.5 trillion, sustaining 5.7 million jobs or 3.79 percent of the workforce.[18]

15 "Bell welcomes Federal Court decision against illicit set-top box providers," Bell Canada, August 12, 2021; https://www.bce.ca/news-and-media/releases/show/bell-welcomes-federal-court-decision-against-illicit-set-top-box-providers; accessed December 31, 2021.

16 Statistics Canada, "Provincial and Territorial Cultural Indicators, 2019," May 27, 2021; https://www150.statcan.gc.ca/n1/daily-quotidien/210527/dq210527b-eng.htm; accessed December 31, 2021.

17 Statistics Canada, "Provincial and Territorial Cultural Indicators, 2020," June 2, 2022; https://www150.statcan.gc.ca/n1/daily-quotidien/220602/dq220602b-eng.htm; accessed November 2, 2022.

18 Robert Stoner and Jessica Dutra, "Copyright Industries in the U.S. Economy: The 2020 Report," International Intellectual Property Alliance, December 14, 2020; https://www.iipa.org/files/uploads/2020/12/2020-IIPA-Report-FINAL-web.pdf; accessed December 31, 2021.

All this contribution to economic welfare is undermined by piracy.

WHAT DRIVES PIRACY?

Just like the corsairs of old, modern copyright pirates are out get something for nothing. While in some cases, the perpetrators are small players, often pirate operators have links to organized crime and generate millions in revenue. On the other hand, some of the businesses that engaged in facilitation of piracy in the early days of the internet, such as Napster, never developed a sustainable business model and never made money. For those organized crime groups reaping the economic benefits of piracy, copyright theft is often viewed as a soft crime, one for which the penalty will likely be much less severe than drug trafficking or other criminal offences. While many cases of piracy are pursued through civil remedies, repeated commercial-scale piracy can also be a criminal offence.

Although those who operate pirate sites derive the most economic benefit, it takes a willing consumer to keep a pirate distributor in business. The motivation for downloaders and streamers of pirated content are several. A 2018 study[19]

19 Government of Canada, "Study of Online Consumption of Copyrighted Content: Attitudes Toward and Prevalence of Copyright Infringement in Canada — Final Report," Innovation, Science and Economic Development Canada, March 30, 2018; https://ised-isde.canada.ca/site/public-opinion-research/en/study-online-consumption-copyrighted-content-attitudes-toward-and-prevalence-copyright-infringement#a01; accessed December 31, 2021.

commissioned by the Department of Innovation, Science and Economic Development in Canada ascribed the following motivations to those who identified as having accessed infringing online content during the past three months:

- It's free (54%)
- It's easy/convenient (40%)
- It's quick (34%)
- It means I can try something before I buy it (19%)
- I can't afford to pay (19%)
- I think legal content is too expensive (11%)
- The content is not available on the legal services that I subscribe to and pay for (11%)

Other reasons included the content not being available in Canada; following the example of friends and family; a belief that industry made too much money; and not wanting to wait for legal content to become available. There was also a small minority who offered excuses like "no one suffers" and "no one ever gets caught."

One way of summarizing this would be to say that motivations range from greed or penury to laziness or ideology. Some of the reasons appear to be justifications for what the individual knows is unacceptable behaviour; others can perhaps be addressed by copyright industries to reduce the attractions of piracy.

HOW TO COMBAT PIRACY

While no business can compete with "free," and while copyright holders have the absolute right to price their works at a level they deem appropriate, common sense indicates that more competitive prices will reduce the attraction of piracy. Greater scale of legitimate offerings presents one way to bring down costs. Availability is another consideration. The film industry is now moving toward simultaneous release in multiple geographic regions, a strategy made possible by the introduction of digital distribution. Shortening exclusive theatrical release windows prior to broader online distribution has also proven to be a successful strategy. New streaming platforms, such as Netflix, less wedded to theatrical release, have also changed industry practices. This said, sometimes rights issues still hinder distribution in certain jurisdictions.

As for the complaint that a consumer needs to subscribe to multiple services to be able to access the full range of content available, that is a reality of not only the content industry but also any industry where competing services are offered. If you want a certain specialty product offered at only one store, that is where you must go to get it. Content is a specialty product — one TV series or film cannot be substituted for another. The only service that offers the possibility of aggregating all content (and even in this case there are many exceptions) is piracy, where content is hijacked. No legitimate business should be expected to compete with those who aggregate content without obtaining licences.

Convenience is another factor that can be used to combat piracy. First, content providers need to make content widely and readily available through various formats and delivery platforms. That is certainly happening. Second, access to pirated content needs to be made inconvenient through measures such as site blocking. Technological protection measures, such as copy and access controls, can also be employed, both to make it easier for subscribers who pay for content (who can be given an easy-to-use "key") and to make it more difficult for those who feel it is their right to help themselves to content produced by others without payment.

A mix of education and enforcement needs to be employed. Education is needed to counter the mistaken impression among many that anything found on the internet should be free for the taking. The argument that knowledge should be free for society's benefit has been advanced by pirates over the centuries, including the piracy of sheet music back in the day.[20] The realities and economics of content creation need to be explained to the public, along with outlining the benefits both to consumers and society generally of maintaining a healthy creative sector. Despite all the education in the world, however, there will still be a small minority who will ignore the law. Just as with the enforcement of traffic laws for the benefit of everyone, so too do copyright laws have to be enforced on occasion.

20 *Piracy*, Johns, pp. 345–48.

SUMMARY

In this chapter, we have looked at the origins and types of content piracy. The use of the term "piracy" to describe infringement of copyright has a long history, and, unfortunately, for some it conveys an image of quasi-acceptable behaviour. Piracy saps the lifeblood of the creative industries, weakens the incentive to create, and undermines the economic benefits produced by copyright industries. The motivations for piracy are primarily economic on the part of both distributors and end users, although availability and convenience are also factors. Industry has responded to many of these challenges, although no legitimate business can compete with "free." A balance of market response and education with targeted enforcement is needed to combat piracy and ensure that creative industries thrive for the benefit of cultural communities, consumers, and the economy.

CHAPTER 5

Piracy:
Three Case Studies

PIRACY AND HYBRID WARFARE: THE CASE OF beIN SPORTS
Piracy can have political overtones and even be used as a form
of hybrid warfare. This new form of war has various dimensions, including social media disinformation campaigns
(particularly to manipulate election results or to create internal dissension), cyberattacks, use of remote vehicles and
drones, use of private armies to seize territories, economic
measures such as sanctions or disruption of supply chains,
and other measures that fall short of outright use of force
or are plausibly deniable. Hybrid warfare is the kind of
deniable warfare engaged in by Russia in its 2014 invasion
of the Crimea or reportedly by the U.S. with cyberwarfare
against Iran's nuclear program. This is the story of a form
of hybrid warfare involving copyright piracy that occurred
between 2017 and 2020 in the Middle East between the
State of Qatar and the Kingdom of Saudi Arabia.

The Gulf states — Kuwait, Bahrain, Qatar, and the United Arab Emirates — are like a hem sewn on the northeastern edges of the Arabian Peninsula, which is dominated by Saudi Arabia. One Gulf state in particular sticks in the craw of the Saudis. This is Qatar, one of the world's largest producers of natural gas, enormously wealthy, host to the 2022 FIFA World Cup, and home of the controversial television network Al-Jazeera. Qatar's ruling family, the Al-Thani dynasty, originally came from a desert area now in Saudi Arabia, and there are still elements of tribal rivalry with the Saud family. More recently, Qatar has challenged Saudi hegemony in the region, particularly through the coverage of controversial issues by state-controlled network Al-Jazeera. Saudi Arabia has broken diplomatic relations with Qatar on more than one occasion, and in 2017 it closed its airspace to Qatar airlines, sought a pan-Arab boycott on docking by Qatari ships, and closed its land border with Qatar.

As part of their "punishment" of Qatar, the Saudis blocked Qatari websites, including Al-Jazeera, and banned Al-Jazeera channels from hotel distribution in the kingdom. The Saudis wanted Al-Jazeera shut down, but that hasn't happened. In fact, Al-Jazeera stuck the knife in by relentlessly covering the shocking murder of Saudi journalist Jamal Khashoggi in the Saudi Consulate in Istanbul. The land border was closed for a time, and there were rumours that the Saudis intended to make the blockage permanent by digging a canal across the Qatari peninsula to sever the state from the mainland.

Into this mix, we throw sports and broadcasting. The leading sports channel in the region is the Qatari-based network beIN Sports. beIN is a global network operating in the Middle East, North Africa, France, Spain, the U.S., Canada, Australia, New Zealand, Turkey, Hong Kong, and several countries in southeast Asia. It is not irrelevant to know that it was formerly known as Al-Jazeera Sports. According to beIN's website, it has "disassociated" from Al-Jazeera; but, while it is legally separate, many still consider it to be part of the Al-Jazeera Media Group. Its exact relationship to Al-Jazeera today is a bit unclear. beIN has been active in acquiring rights to many sports, particularly soccer, the most popular sport in the Middle East. It has a terrific lineup, including UEFA championships, English Premier League, Spain's La Liga, Germany's Bundesliga, and other top-calibre soccer. It is a must-have for soccer fans and was widely available in Saudi Arabia until the 2017 Saudi-Qatari rupture.

Given the no-holds-barred state of Saudi-Qatar relations, plus the fact that Saudi Arabia has more than ten times Qatar's population, the Saudi leadership had no intention of allowing a Qatari sports channel to get rich by providing must-have sports coverage to the millions of Saudis who follow soccer. The Saudis are accustomed to getting their own way, but the problem was that beIN Sports had tied up all the broadcast rights in the region. Even if there was a decent Saudi sports channel (which there wasn't), the Saudis could not get major league soccer rights for the Middle East. The solution for the Saudis was to first block beIN Sports to the widest extent possible so that it couldn't reach Saudi consumers and then allow beIN's signal to be pirated and distributed illegally to Saudi (and other) audiences. This new service, called BeoutQ, was carried on Arabsat, the regional satellite broadcasting provider. Arabsat, owned by the Arab League (with the Saudi government as the dominant shareholder), is headquartered in Riyadh. The new competing pirate service would damage beIN's business, but more importantly, it would strike back at the Qatari regime. Like much in hybrid warfare, it had to be plausibly deniable, especially since the U.S. is the top military backer of the Saudi regime — and the U.S. happens to be a strong advocate for the respect of intellectual property rights.

Each year, the United States Trade Representative issues a report commenting on the state of intellectual property protection in foreign countries. The report for 2019 criticized the state of intellectual property protection in Saudi Arabia and, using careful language, commented, "BeoutQ, an illicit service for pirated content whose signal is reportedly carried by Saudi Arabia–based satellite provider Arabsat, continues to be widely available in Saudi Arabia and throughout the Middle East and Europe ... While Saudi officials have confirmed the illegal nature of BeoutQ's activities and claim to be addressing this issue by seizing BeoutQ set-top boxes, such devices nevertheless continue to be widely available and are generally unregulated in

Saudi Arabia. Saudi Arabia also has not taken sufficient steps to address the purported role of Arabsat in facilitating BeoutQ's piracy activities."[1]

The hybrid warfare worked for a while. beIN Sports laid off three hundred staff in Qatar, a fifth of its Qatar-based workforce, citing a drop in profits as a result of Saudi piracy. While beIN Sports and Qatar were not happy about the widespread content piracy by BeoutQ, neither were the sports leagues, who were concerned that one of their best customers had just lost a large chunk of its market to a rogue operation. The leagues wanted to sue, but neither beIN nor various football associations were able to secure legal representation in Saudi Arabia due to a sudden and unexplained dearth of available legal counsel to take on the case.

In desperation, beIN appealed to the Qatari government for help, and Qatar filed a case against Saudi Arabia at the World Trade Organization, with other WTO members (Australia, Bahrain, Brazil, Canada, China, the EU, Japan, Norway, Russia, Singapore, Ukraine, the UAE, and the U.S.) joining and submitting briefs as interested third parties. Only member governments can bring WTO cases. On June 16, 2020, a WTO panel found that Qatar had clearly established that the pirated BeoutQ network was operated by individuals within the criminal jurisdiction of

1 Office of the U.S. Trade Representative, "2019 Special 301 Report", p. 57; https://ustr.gov/sites/default/files/2019_Special_301_Report.pdf; accessed December 26, 2021.

Saudi Arabia and that the kingdom had not only failed to take any action against them but had prevented a Qatari company from exercising civil enforcement of its intellectual property rights.[2] The panel instructed Saudi Arabia to "bring its measures into conformity with its obligations under the TRIPS agreement." (TRIPS, as we have seen earlier, deals with intellectual property disputes under the WTO framework.)[3]

Not coincidentally, shortly after the WTO decision, the Saudi Authority for Intellectual Property announced that it would be blocking 231 websites that violated intellectual property law, including a number that distributed illicit streaming devices. BeoutQ's direct satellite broadcast service had been shut down in late 2019 but continued to be available through these devices via the internet. In addition, the president of the Saudi Arabia Football Federation wrote to the Union of European Football Associations, the English Premier League, the international football federation FIFA, and the International Olympic Committee acknowledging that Saudi Arabia had a responsibility to fight broadcast piracy and respect intellectual property rights.

2 World Trade Organization, "Saudi Arabia-Measures Concerning the Protection of Intellectual Property Rights," https://www.wto.org/english /tratop_e/dispu_e/567r_e.pdf; accessed December 26, 2021.

3 Under WTO rules, a country can accept or challenge a panel ruling. The Saudis appealed the ruling based on the contention that their actions were justified by the WTO's national security exemption. That appeal has still not been decided, but the Saudis have removed the irritant by ensuring that BeoutQ is out of business.

Whatever the motivation for ending the dispute — whether it was the WTO decision, U.S. pressure, or, as some have suggested, the interest of the chairman of the Saudi sovereign wealth fund, Crown Prince Mohammed bin Salman, who wanted to purchase a major Premier League team, Newcastle United[4] — it is now over, and sports piracy has ceased to be a tool of hybrid warfare in the Middle East.

STATE-SANCTIONED PIRACY: QUEEN ANNE'S REVENGE

While copyright law falls within the prerogative of the federal government in the U.S., hearkening back to the Copyright Act of 1790, the individual U.S. states also used to legislate in the copyright area. The 1976 U.S. Copyright Act established federal primacy once and for all, but the states still play a role. One of the most controversial aspects of this role is the claim of state governments and state institutions to immunity from federal copyright law with respect to actions taken by them as part of their official duties. Thus, some state universities have used state immunity as a defence against charges of copyright infringement brought by educational publishers. The most egregious example of a state government thumbing its nose at U.S.

---

4 Areeb Ullah, "Newcastle takeover: Why Qatar's beIN Sports was key to Saudi deal," *Middle East Eye*, October 8, 2021; https://www.middleeasteye.net/news/newcastle-united-takeover-saudi-qatar-bein-why-key; accessed December 26, 2021.

federal copyright law is the case of Allen v Cooper.[5] Roy A. Cooper is the governor of North Carolina. Rick Allen is a filmmaker and owner of Nautilus Productions.

It started in 1996, when a company named Intersal, Inc. located the remains of the *Queen Anne's Revenge* (QAR), the ship of the infamous pirate Edward Teach, commonly known as Blackbeard, off the North Carolina coast. It had sunk there in 1718 after a naval engagement. Shortly after discovering the wreck, the company signed a memorandum of agreement with the North Carolina Department of Cultural Resources,[6] which, according to Intersal, granted the company, among other things, the "exclusive right ... to produce, co-produce or commission a documentary film (or series of films) detailing the story of the research, search for, discovery, and salvage of QAR." A film company, Nautilus Productions, was engaged to be the official video crew to film the underwater salvage operation, and that footage was seen in over a dozen documentaries broadcast worldwide by ABC, BBC, CNN, Discovery Channel, National Geographic, PBS, Smithsonian Channel, and others. Nautilus Productions claims that it is "the exclusive owner and licensor of footage from Black-

5 Supreme Court of the United States, Allen et al. v Governor of North Carolina, et al., 18–77; March 23, 2020; https://www.supremecourt.gov/opinions/19pdf/18-877_dc8f.pdf; accessed February 3, 2022 (Allen v Cooper).

6 "Queen Anne's Revenge Project," NC Department of Natural and Cultural Resources, https://www.qaronline.org/; accessed January 1, 2022,

beard the Pirate's flagship, the *Queen Anne's Revenge*."[7]

Then things began to break down between the Department of Cultural Resources and Intersal, resulting in a dispute over the use of images of the underwater ship. Under the terms of a settlement agreement reached in 2013 between the department, Intersal, and Nautilus, the film company and its owner, filmmaker Rick Allen, received $15,000 to settle alleged copyright infringement. But this was not the end of the dispute, and in July 2015, Intersal brought an $8-million lawsuit against the department for contract violation. The state responded in August 2015 by passing House Bill 184,[8] known colloquially as "Blackbeard's Law," which stated, among other things, "all photographs, video recordings, or other documentary materials of a derelict vessel or shipwreck or its contents, relics, artifacts, or historic materials in the custody of any agency of North Carolina government or its subdivisions shall be a public record ... [and] there shall be no limitation on the use of or no requirement to alter any such photograph, video recordings, or other documentary material, and any such provision in any agreement, permit, or license shall be void and unenforceable as a matter of public policy." In plain language, the North Carolina legislature passed

---

7 "Blackbeard's Queen Anne's Revenge Shipwreck Project," http://nautilusproductions.com/projects/queen-annes-revenge; accessed January 1, 2022.

8 General Assembly of North Carolina, Session Law 2015-218, House Bill 184; https://www.ncleg.net/Sessions/2015/Bills/House/PDF/H184v7.pdf; accessed January 1, 2022.

a law that claimed that if the subject matter of the work of a photographer, videographer, or filmmaker happens to be a derelict vessel or shipwreck under the jurisdiction of the State of North Carolina, all such work shall be in the public domain with no requirement to respect the author's watermarks or other identifying marks of ownership. The legislation has the effect of nullifying any existing claims to copyright or licence agreements going forward.

After the passage of "Blackbeard's Law," the state resumed infringement both online and in print. Allen issued takedown notices that were ignored. Allen then sued the Department of Cultural Resources. North Carolina argued that it had sovereign immunity under the Eleventh Amendment of the U.S. Constitution and could not be sued for its actions. While there is no doubt that U.S. states have sovereign immunity in most matters as a result of this amendment, there is the competing requirement under Article 1 of the U.S. Constitution that grants authors and inventors for a limited term the exclusive right of protection for "their respective Writings and Discoveries." In accordance with Article 1, Congress also enacted, in 1990, the Copyright Remedy Clarification Act,[9] which provides that states and state officers "shall not be immune, under the Eleventh Amendment of the Constitution of the United States or under other doctrine of sovereign immunity, from suit in

9   U.S. Congress, Statute at Large 104, Stat 2749, Public Law 101-553 (11/15/1990); https://www.congress.gov/bill/101st-congress/house-bill/3045/text; accessed January 1, 2022.

Federal court by any person … for a violation of any of the exclusive rights of a copyright owner provided by [federal law]."

The suit went all the way to the Supreme Court of the United States, which agreed to decide whether North Carolina's state sovereignty, as granted by the Eleventh Amendment of 1795, trumped the Copyright Remedy Clarification Act.

The Supreme Court reached its decision on March 23, 2020, finding that the 1990 congressional legislation did not remove North Carolina's sovereign immunity. North Carolina got away with piracy! Was this Queen Anne's revenge? Given the importance of this ruling for copyright, it is surely ironic that the shipwreck in question is named after the British sovereign for whom the Statute of Anne, the seminal piece of British legislation that established the copyright of authors, is also named.

Queen Anne may yet get her revenge when it comes to stopping the piracy practiced by the State of North Carolina. When it reached its decision also also in March to uphold the state's claim of sovereign immunity (based largely on precedent, plus the fact that congressional legislation should be allowed to abrogate provisions of the U.S. Constitution in only the most extreme and limited circumstances, and only when such actions are intentional and constitutional), the court nonetheless offered a lifeline to copyright holders. It wrote that when Congress passed its legislation in 1990, it "likely did not appreciate the importance of linking the scope of its abrogation to the redress or prevention of unconstitutional injuries — and of creating a legislative record to back up that connection." Therefore, said the court, "going forward, Congress will know these rules. And under them, if it detects violations of due process, then it may enact a proportionate response. That kind of tailored statute can effectively stop States from behaving as copyright pirates. Even while respecting constitutional limits, it can bring digital Blackbeards to justice."[10]

To date, the U.S. Congress has not picked up the challenge of curtailing the abuse of copyright by state governments, but the U.S. Copyright Office has been mandated to study the problem and bring forth a report. That 117-page study, "Copyright and State Sovereign Immunity" (August 2021), concluded that "state infringement represents a legitimate concern for copyright owners" and recommended that Congress take action.[11] In future, if Congress brings forth legislation to deal with this issue, it should be able to pass a bulletproof law that will withstand Supreme Court scrutiny. State-sponsored copyright piracy should then come to an end. Queen Anne will have finally got her (copyright) revenge. That would be sweet irony.

10 Allen v Cooper, p. 16; https://www.supremecourt.gov/opinions/19pdf/18-877_dc8f.pdf.

11 U.S. Copyright Office, "Copyright and State Sovereign Immunity," August 2021; https://www.copyright.gov/policy/state-sovereign-immunity/Sovereign%20Immunity%20Report%20final.pdf; accessed November 2, 2022.

PIRACY IN CHINA

Whenever there is a discussion about content piracy and trade in counterfeit goods, China inevitably comes up. According to the Organisation for Economic Co-operation and Development (OECD),[12] China and Hong Kong continue to be by far the largest source countries for counterfeit and pirated goods. What is the reason for this? Sheer size, local "initiative," and economic and cultural factors should all be considered. China is a vast country, and despite centralized political control through the Chinese Communist Party and central government organs, many provincial and county officials are slow to respond to central directives. This has led to flourishing markets for pirated and counterfeit products, both physical and online, despite laws to the contrary. There has been an improvement in the enforcement of copyright law in China as local stakeholders have invested in content and have used local courts to enforce their copyrights against domestic transgressors. But infringement of foreign copyrights continues to be a problem, an issue that has its roots in Chinese history.

Respect for copyright in China, or the lack thereof, has been a recurring topic over the years. For example, the Office of the United States Trade Representative (USTR) Special 301 Report on China issued in April 2020 stated, "It is critical that China address major deficiencies in its

---

12   OECD EUIPO (2019), *Trends in Trade in Counterfeit and Pirated Goods, Illicit Trade*, OECD Publishing, Paris/European Union Intellectual Property Office; https://doi.org/10.1787/g2g9f533-en; accessed January 13, 2022.

copyright framework, such as the lack of deterrent civil damages, ineffective criminal enforcement, and the failure to provide protection against the unauthorized transmission of sports and other live broadcasts."[13]

The report also raised concerns around digital piracy related to distribution of unauthorized audiovisual content and dissemination of unauthorized copies of scientific, technical, and medical journal articles and academic texts, as well as China's failure to take sustained action against websites, devices, or apps that offer or facilitate access to unlicensed content.[14]

The reason for China's lack of robust intellectual property protection, including in the area of copyright, has been attributed to several factors. A common academic view seeks to explain China's lack of respect for intellectual property as a cultural phenomenon. Here is a good example of this line of argument, based on supposed Confucian values: "The primary orientation of Chinese culture is toward mutual reliance ... One distinction is that all forms of creativity are for the collective; any copying or imitating is a high form of flattery ..."[15]

---

13 Office of the United States Trade Representative, "2020 Special 301 Report", April 2020, p. 46; https://ustr.gov/sites/default/files/2020_Special _301_Report.pdf; accessed January 13, 2022.

14 2020 Special 301 Report, pp. 43–44.

15 Jessica Gisclair, "The Dissonance between Culture and Intellectual Property in China," *Southeast Review of Asian Studies*, Volume 30 (2008), pp. 182–87; http://citeseerx.ist.psu.edu/viewdoc/download?-doi=10.1.1.538.9440&rep=rep1&type=pdf; accessed January 13, 2022.

It is true that some Confucian values still permeate traditional Chinese worldviews, but do they really explain rampant copyright violations in China? Are copyright pirates in China motivated by a desire to flatter the artists they are stealing from? I doubt it.

Another take comes from what is often considered the definitive work on the subject of Chinese copyright and its traditions, William P. Alford's *To Steal a Book is an Elegant Offense*.[16] In this widely known work, the author postulates some reasons for China's weak copyright protection, reaching back far into history. At the risk of oversimplifying, Alford's main thesis is that while China appears to have had a form of copyright and trademark protection extending as far back as the Tang dynasty (618–907 CE), these regulations were primarily intended to protect the power and prerogatives of the state rather than the works of individual artists or authors. Accordingly, it was forbidden to reproduce government works on astronomy, the civil service examinations, and other matters considered sensitive for purposes of security and censorship, but when it came to private ownership of materials, there was no legal tradition of protecting original works. Indeed, Alford points out, "the Confucian disdain for commerce fostered an ideal, even if not always realized in practice, that true scholars wrote for edification and moral renewal rather than profit."

16 William P. Alford, *To Steal a Book is an Elegant Offense*, Stanford, 1995.

While a true Confucian scholar might disdain profit, the merchant class were entrepreneurial and aggressive in their drive for profit, including in the publishing industry. They did not hesitate to reprint whatever they could (avoiding the pirating of government publications that would land them in trouble), yet at the same time they devised a sort of code that regulated their conduct toward each other. When it came to pirating foreign materials, however, that was another matter. Foreigners were fair game.

At the end of the nineteenth century, the Qing Empire was on the verge of collapse. The Chinese had been thrashed by the Japanese in the Sino-Japanese War of 1894–95 (which led to the Japanese occupation of Taiwan), and European powers were tearing at the hem of China, nibbling off little pieces for themselves. Chinese reformers recognized that China needed to adopt some western values, including promotion of modernization and innovation. The development of intellectual property laws was considered one element of this. At the same time, the European powers were keen to impose on China (at gunpoint, if necessary) various obligations to protect their own economic interests, including copyright. As a result, several bilateral treaties were signed between China and European countries and the U.S. regarding intellectual property protection, although the Chinese were slow to enact these obligations into law, and even slower to attempt any enforcement. For example, while the U.S. and China signed a bilateral treaty providing for reciprocal protection of copyrights and trademarks in 1903, the Chinese did not get around to enacting their first copyright law until 1911. That was the same year the Qing Empire collapsed, and China entered an extended period of internal turmoil. Given the prevailing political situation, enforcement of copyright was not a high priority for the new republican government.

The lack of statute law protecting copyright under the Qing Empire was a major obstacle and is advanced as one reason for widespread tolerance of book piracy in China. Foreign publishers were regularly pirated, but did this occur because of a lack of understanding of the fundamentals of copyright, or was it simply a case of commercial opportunism? An interesting new work, *Pirates and Publishers: A Social History of Copyright in Modern China*,[17] calls into question much of the conventional wisdom regarding Chinese attitudes to copyright. It suggests that Chinese publishers, booksellers, and authors were well aware of the importance of copyright at the beginning of the twentieth century and later, at least insofar as it applied to them and not to foreigners. Professor Fei-Hsien Wang argues that contrary to common belief, copyright was not a foreign doctrine imposed on China by western powers with little regard for Chinese cultural and social traditions. Given the absence of enforceable statutory law in this area, Chinese authors, booksellers, and publishers developed

17 Fei-Hsien Wang, *Pirates and Publishers: A Social History of Copyright in Modern China*, Princeton, 2019.

their own form of copyright, which played a crucial role in its growth and eventual institutionalization in China. These individuals enforced what they viewed as copyright to justify their profit, protect their books, and crack down on piracy by others.

How did they do this? In the absence of the existence of a copyright law (in the period prior to 1911) or the enforcement of said law (for many years after the law was enacted), the Chinese book trade established guilds with their own registration, code of enforcement, tracking system, piracy investigators, and sanctions. This was not dissimilar to the guilds formed by London booksellers back in the seventeenth century.[18] Wang cites the case of Ginn & Co, the noted U.S. publisher who brought suit in 1911 in Shanghai against the Shanghai Commercial Press, which had reprinted Ginn's history textbook without authorization. Representing Ginn was T.R. Jernigan, a noted commercial lawyer and former U.S. consul general in Shanghai. Jernigan faced significant legal obstacles because the new copyright law did not apply to foreigners (despite bilateral treaties being one of the reasons for passage of the law), so he argued on the basis of common law that since Chinese publishers respected and enforced copyright amongst themselves, the local practices should apply to the defendants in the Ginn case. He did not prevail, but the incident helps shed light on an informal copyright code

18 Johns, *Piracy: The Intellectual Property Wars from Gutenberg to Gates*, pp. 24–29.

that existed in China — but for Chinese only, and then only some Chinese.

Shanghai was the centre of the Chinese publishing and bookselling industry, and naturally this is where the copyright guilds emerged. There were two main groups: the Shanghai Booksellers' Guild and the Shanghai Booksellers' Trade Association. Titles were registered based on the original printing blocks (*shudi*, or master copy) or type plates or paper stereotypes for letterpress printing. Generally, members of the guild respected each other's *banquan* (the word used today to translate "copyright," which can be literally translated as "the authority or power to print"), but if there were disputes, the guild would mediate. It would also dole out punishments, such as fining offenders and burning copies along with the pirated *shudi*. Sometimes there were negotiated solutions in which pirates could pay to have their editions authorized.

While Shanghai was the main commercial centre, it had rivals in Beijing (known at the time as Beiping after the national capital moved to Nanjing). The booksellers and publishers in Beijing did not belong to the Shanghai guilds, nor did they pay them much heed. Although China was technically unified under the KMT regime in Nanjing, local authorities had considerable power, and the national government had a difficult time in enforcing its writ. Local "initiative" was the order of the day, and Beijing became the book pirate capital of China. Again, there are some similarities with the early book trade in Britain, where

Scottish printers refused to recognize the monopoly rights of London printers.

In the early 1930s, the Beijing representatives of the leading Shanghai publishers petitioned the Beiping city government to act against open piracy, even describing several "notorious markets" (echoing the description in USTR's annual Special 301 Reports today) where pirated works were sold openly. Like today, there would be a raid, and then the zeal of the local authorities would fade. The Shanghai publishers realized that they needed their own people on the ground to ferret out the pirates, and so they formed their own team of private investigators. The investigators would build a case and present it to the Beiping authorities, who might or might not act, particularly since most of the *banquan* was not a legally registered copyright but rather the unofficial copyright registered with the Shanghai guilds. Moreover, as the author points out, while to the Shanghai publishers the Beijing booksellers were pirates, to the local authorities they were business leaders who deserved to be sheltered.

The experience of the Shanghai publishers from the early 1900s until the late 1930s, when much of China was taken over by the Japanese, is eerily reflective of the experience of many western copyright holders in China in recent years. Even today, despite the presence of strict laws against copyright infringement and other forms of intellectual property theft, pirated and counterfeit goods are sold openly both online and physically, often in so-called notorious markets. Private companies and associations have resorted to hiring private investigators to gather evidence to bring before Chinese courts. On occasion, there is a big bust or anti-piracy ("strike hard") campaign, which then peters out once the period for the campaign is over. Frequently, local authorities are not interested in pursuing intellectual property crimes or are actively engaged in protecting local interests engaged in pirating or counterfeiting activities, which they see as contributing to local economic activity. In short, nothing much has changed.

It is revealing to see the similarity between the experience of the Shanghai publishers in Beijing more than eighty years ago and the struggles faced today by both foreign and Chinese copyright holders seeking to protect their rights. For the Shanghai booksellers of the early twentieth century, self-help was the only way to succeed in a country with weak copyright laws and limited or no will or ability to enforce them. At the same time, the efforts of the Shanghai publishing and bookselling guilds clearly establish that Chinese merchants were well aware of copyright and used it to promote and protect their economic interests. They did not subscribe to vague Confucian theories of sharing the common good of knowledge or producing content for its own sake. They were hardheaded businesspeople who not only took collective action to protect their own copyright but, when they could get away with it, had no qualms about appropriating foreign content without payment.

Collective behaviour is normally rooted in cultural traditions and beliefs, and it would be wrong to say that Confucian values have no sway in China today. There may even be a residual belief among some Chinese scholars that the notion of copyright to protect individual economic interests and moral rights (which in turn incentivizes more creation) is at odds with traditional collective Confucian beliefs. But that is a very thin cloak to use as justification for widespread intellectual property theft in China. A look back at a century or more of Chinese history shows that Chinese entrepreneurs were well able to grasp the importance of copyright and employ it to advance and protect their own economic interests. Where they failed to respect copyright, as in the case of foreign works unprotected by weak Chinese laws, they did so knowing full well what they were doing for commercial gain, pure and simple. Confucius the scholar may be turning in his grave, but Cai Shen, the god of wealth, is laughing all the way to the bank.

SUMMARY

This chapter has outlined three case studies to illustrate the reach of copyright internationally, its complexity, and how it can affect both international relations and internal constitutional and political issues.

CHAPTER 6

Contested Uses: Conflicting Interpretations Around Legal Uses of a Copyrighted Work

BLATANT BOOK PIRACY is relatively rare today, although some self-published authors have found their more successful e-books pirated by others on Amazon. (It is a truism that only successful books are pirated.) Other forms of unauthorized use have also sprung up, and there is little doubt that new ones will arise in the future. These uses are unauthorized in the sense that they have not been sanctioned by the author or copyright holder through either a licensing agreement or other form of permission such as a Creative Commons licence. Whether they constitute piracy is a matter of opinion. In the final analysis, that decision depends on a legal interpretation. Piracy involves blatant disregard of the law, whereas other forms of infringement and unauthorized use usually arise from differences of interpretation as to what is legal.

In Chapter 3, we examined the many circumstances in which copyright law does not apply: public domain, specified exceptions, court interpretations as to what constitutes fair use or fair dealing, non-substantial use, and other limitations. While some exceptions to copyright, such as works in the public domain, are usually clear and non-controversial, others are much less so. There are differences of interpretation depending on whether the issue is looked at from the perspective of a copyright holder who wants to exercise their rights or of a user who chooses not to acquire a licence. In many cases, the motivation for the latter is economic, but in some it is ideological, a belief — mistaken, in my view — that copyright locks up works and denies access to the public. This is looking at the question of public access through the wrong lens, because without the incentive to create works provided by copyright, there would be no works to access.

While legislation establishes the terms and forms of protection afforded by copyright laws, despite the best efforts of legislators, there are grey areas. In many countries, a final determination on a case-by-case basis remains the domain of the courts. Often, court decisions are appealed, sometimes ending up at a country's supreme court, with split decisions being not infrequent. Copyright holders often seek injunctions to block unauthorized uses they consider infringements of copyright. Litigation can take years and can be enormously expensive. Individual authors and small copyright holders usually do not have the financial wherewithal to protect their copyright in this way; as a result, only a small proportion of disputes are actually litigated, but those cases help provide the guidelines that set the boundaries of the playing field.

The following cases have been chosen to illustrate the nature of this process. Some of the cases have been decided by the courts. Others, at the time of writing, are still in process.

GOOGLE BOOKS

Back in the early 2000s, Google began its book digitization project, aiming to eventually digitize and make available electronically every book ever published. Whether a book was under copyright or not was of no concern for Google, but this stance quickly earned the ire of authors and publishers. Google took the position that authors could opt out of the digitization project. Authors took the view that Google needed to obtain their permission. Google argued that its motive was to make books more widely available, but digitization of content owned by others also helped to drive Google's business model by attracting more users, thus increasing advertising revenues.

Google was sued by the Authors Guild, the Association of American Publishers, and others. While a settlement was reached with the publishers, the case brought by the authors went to trial. To avoid charges of copyright infringement, Google agreed to display only portions of books (up to 20 percent), not the full work. From Google's perspective, this would benefit authors by making their work more available and would entice readers to make a purchase, but in many instances, the excerpts made available by Google provided all that a researcher or reader needed, thus substituting the free excerpt for a likely purchase of the book. Despite this potential impact on the economic exploitability of the work, U.S. courts ultimately found that Google's actions constituted fair use on the basis that Google's use was transformative.[1] Transformation has been interpreted in U.S. law to mean that something new has been added, providing a further purpose or different character while not substituting for the original use of the work.[2]

THE INTERNET ARCHIVE AND CONTROLLED DIGITAL LENDING

A similar controversy regarding unauthorized digitization of copyrighted works arose from the actions of the Internet Archive, a self-described "non-profit library of millions of free books, movies, software, music, websites, and more"[3] based in San Francisco. The Archive preserves material on the internet through its Wayback Machine, where earlier versions of websites can be accessed. It also undertakes

1 https://www.authorsguild.org/where-we-stand/authors-guild-v-google/; accessed December 31, 2021.

2 U.S. Copyright Office, "More Information on Fair Use," last updated May 2021; https://www.copyright.gov/fair-use/more-info.html; accessed January 2, 2022.

3 https://archive.org/; accessed December 31, 2021.

widespread digitization of books, regardless of whether they are in copyright or the author has granted permission. The Archive has championed a legally disputed concept known as controlled digital lending whereby digitized copies of books are loaned by the Archive's own "Open Library" or partner libraries. The lending model, which has no basis in law, depends on a library owning and retaining in storage at least one physical version of the work while the digitized copy is out on loan. If two digital copies are loaned simultaneously, two physical copies must be held at the institution. This is referred to as the "owned to loan" ratio. Despite the limitation on the number of digital copies in circulation at any one time, publishers consider the unauthorized digitization to be a violation of their digital rights to works, given that they often produce and license digital editions of their works to libraries and individual users. In other words, the digital copy of the physical book competes with and substitutes for a licensed digital edition or e-book.

While publishers weren't happy with the Internet Archive's controlled digital lending model, worse was yet to come. In 2020, the Archive declared it was creating a "National Emergency Library" because of the COVID-19 pandemic. It opened the floodgates to unrestricted digital lending by suspending the requirement that the number of digital copies on loan should match the number of physical copies it held. It was also not clear if the Archive actually held physical copies of all the works it was lending digitally.

The response of authors, through the Authors Guild, was outrage. The Guild pointed out that the Archive had no rights to the books, including no right to reproduce them digitally nor to give them away indiscriminately without consent of the publisher or author.[4] At time of writing, the Internet Archive is the subject of a lawsuit brought by several major publishers against its controlled digital lending practices.[5] On March 24, 2023, a New York federal judge ruled that the Internet Archive's controlled digital lending practices did not constitute fair use and that the Archive is liable for copyright infringement. At time of publication, the decision is under appeal.

USE OF NEWS SNIPPETS BY INTERNET PLATFORMS

A current issue being played out in several countries, including Canada, is to the extent to which internet platforms such as Google and Facebook should be able to use excerpts of news content and links to such content without licensing that content from news publishers. Google News and Google Search both use headlines and small excerpts of news content to highlight news stories. As for Facebook, news stories are often posted by users, and in some cases by the news outlets themselves. The platforms argue they are

4 https://www.authorsguild.org/industry-advocacy/internet-archives-uncontrolled-digital-lending/; accessed December 31, 2021.

5 Hachette Book Group Inc v Internet Archive; https://www.courtlistener.com/docket/17211300/hachette-book-group-inc-v-internet-archive/; accessed November 3, 2022.

providing news publishers with a free service and greater exposure, driving more viewers to access their content. News providers counter that their content is being used without permission to drive viewership on the platforms, thus leading to increased digital ad sales. It is not irrelevant to note that traditional media, especially print media, is facing a crisis in many countries as advertisers and ad revenues migrate from newspapers and magazines to online platforms. The issue is further complicated by the fact that Google News, for example, a service that aggregates news coverage, does not specifically sell ads against that content. Facebook likewise argues that news content constitutes a relatively small proportion of the content on its platform. A key question is whether news content attracts viewers who then stay on the platform for other purposes, where they are subsequently exposed to advertising.

The question of whether news content should enjoy copyright protection has a long history.[6] In Tudor and Stuart England, prior to the enactment of the first copyright law in 1710, the rights to publish certain forms of news (prices of commodities, deaths, news from abroad) were granted as licensed monopolies. Not surprisingly, others not awarded the prized licences argued that they too should be able to report the news, given the public's interest.

---

6 Much of the information in the following paragraphs has been drawn from the comprehensive work on this subject, *Who Owns the News* by Professor Will Slauter. See Will Slauter, *Who Owns the News*, Stanford University Press, 2019; https://www.sup.org/books/title/?id=29452; accessed January 2, 2022.

After the passage of the Statute of Anne in 1710, the battle over copyright and news in Britain was launched. The argument was made that those who had acquired the news through their own efforts and expense merited protection (a monopoly on the news they had so laboriously obtained) for a limited period to allow them to harvest the fruits of their labour. Their work was not original but deserved protection under the "sweat of the brow" doctrine. Copyright was one potential means to achieve this protection.

But there were many opposed to granting news monopolies, especially those who benefitted from the free ride. They argued that news is a public good and that the facts constituting news cannot be protected. This reflects the legal position today; facts cannot be copyrighted. The 1886 Berne Convention, the first international copyright treaty, explicitly excluded "news of the day" from copyright protection, an exclusion maintained to this day in Berne's revised twentieth-century text. However, back in the eighteenth century, the factual news of the day was not always readily available, and in many cases, it had to be obtained through considerable effort.

As an example, if Ruritania declares war on Grand Fenwick, that is a fact. But in earlier times, this fact would only become known because a major paper, let's call it the *London Morning Standard*, maintained a correspondent in the capital of one of those faraway places. That correspondent, on learning of the declaration of war, hired a coach and driver to take his dispatch to the nearest seaport, where it was entrusted to the captain of the fastest ship available. Upon arrival in England, the captain conveyed the news report to a dispatch rider, who rode posthaste to enable the *Standard* to break the news in its morning edition. The *Standard* had a scoop, but only for a few hours because when the evening and provincial papers came out, they simply rewrote or copied the story from the *Standard*, sometimes with attribution, sometimes not. There is a vague analogy here to internet platforms profiting from the hard work of professional journalists and publishers without payment while selling advertising against the free content.

One solution in the eighteenth century might have involved extending copyright law to cover content in newspapers, although the Statute of Anne was conceived of primarily for literary works. Despite action by some owners to gain copyright protection for newspaper or magazine content by entering editions at Stationers' Hall (a requirement for copyright protection), most publishers freely reprinted content obtained from rival papers. The prevailing business practices did not support exclusivity. Almost all editors engaged in some form of copying (and took pride in their selection of what to copy).

"Scissors and paste" remained a common practice in newspaper publishing in both Britain and the U.S. through much of the nineteenth century, but lack of attribution was considered by many to be plagiarism. However, by the late nineteenth century, with the advent of the telegraph and press associations that led to pooling of content, attitudes began to change. By the early twentieth century in Britain, a series of court rulings had confirmed that newspaper articles could be protected by copyright, but, as is the case today, a distinction was made between the facts of news (not protected) and the expression of those facts (subject to copyright protection). Attempts to establish a special limited-duration (eighteen to forty-eight hours) copyright protection for news were unsuccessful. In the 1911 Imperial Copyright Act of the UK, fair dealing was introduced, allowing portions of copyrighted works to be reproduced for purposes of research, criticism, review, or newspaper summary. In the U.S., with the formation of press associations, the thrust was to protect exclusivity in news through competition law. The U.S. Supreme Court ruled it was unfair competition to use the exclusive content (hot news) of another agency until such time as the exclusivity was no longer commercially exploitable.[7]

The advent of radio brought another challenge and a struggle over who could control the news. The situation played out in different ways in different countries. In Britain, the BBC was granted a government charter and a broadcast monopoly (which lasted until 1972 in radio), but initially its ability to cover news was heavily restricted.[8] Its

7 International News Service v Associated Press, 248 U.S. 215 (1918); https://supreme.justia.com/cases/federal/us/248/215/; accessed February 3, 2022.

8 "The BBC Takes to the Airwaves," http://news.bbc.co.uk/aboutbbcnews /spl/hi/history/noflash/html/1920s.stm; accessed January 2, 2022.

news coverage had to be drawn from wire service copy, and no news broadcasts were permitted before 7:00 p.m. to avoid competing with the newspapers for subscribers. As a publicly funded government monopoly, it did not compete with newspapers for advertising.

In the U.S., broadcasting remained in private hands (as it was initially in Britain) and did seek advertising dollars. While some newspaper publishers acquired broadcast licences, others did not. This set the stage for competing views of whether radio should be allowed to broadcast news. Originally, many broadcasters simply read newspaper headlines on the air (remember, facts are not protected by copyright). Many newspapers tried to restrict what material broadcasters could use, thus beginning the so-called press-radio war of the 1930s. The two major U.S. radio networks at the time, NBC and CBS, initially agreed to restrict news broadcasts to two five-minute broadcasts a day, one no earlier than 9:30 a.m. (to protect the morning papers) and one no earlier than 9:00 p.m. (to protect the evening dailies). The brief broadcasts were to whet the appetite of listeners to go out and buy papers. The networks also agreed to give up their own news gathering operations and instead to receive copy from the Associated Press. This agreement (the Biltmore Agreement of 1933)[9] lasted less than two years before it began to fall apart, primarily because independent radio stations refused to play

9 Gwenyth L. Jackaway, *Radio's Challenge to the Newspapers, 1924–1939*, Westport CN and London, Praeger, 1995, pp. 27–28.

the game. They decided to broadcast news at the time and in the format that suited their listeners and advertisers. News was and is an elusive commodity to corral.

While attempts to monopolize the news were unsuccessful because of the generic nature of factual information, there is no question that news reporting can be protected as intellectual property. It is the essence of the idea/expression dichotomy in copyright. An investigative news report, carefully researched and written, perhaps illustrated with exclusive photos, is certainly the expression of what that news item is about and is protectable by copyright. But what about snippets and headlines? The U.S. Copyright Office in its guidance document notes that copyright does not protect "names, titles, slogans, or short phrases."[10] We have already seen in Chapter 1, however, that the amount of text copied may not be the determining factor in deciding whether a use was substantial or not. A qualitative assessment must also be made. Could an argument be made that a carefully crafted headline, created with skill and originality, qualitatively captures the essence of the facts being reported? Indeed, as mentioned in Chapter 3, that argument was made in a dispute between the French news agency AFP and Google, resulting in a licensing agreement in 2007 between the two, allowing Google to use AFP headlines and photos.

Recently, the European Union brought forth directives to deal with this issue, creating a press publication

10   U.S. Copyright Office, "What Does Copyright Protect?", https://www.copyright.gov/help/faq/faq-protect.html; accessed January 2, 2022.

right under Article 15 of the EU Copyright Directive.[11] This article confers upon news publishers an ancillary or neighbouring right, similar to copyright but valid for only two years from the date of publication. The intent of the directive is to empower publishers to negotiate with the dominant digital platforms. EU member states are required to pass national legislation to bring their laws into conformity with the EU directive. France has already done so, leading to a major confrontation with Google, in which Google was fined €500 million for failing to negotiate in good faith with French news publishers.[12] Google has now reached licensing agreements with most French publishers in a deal that is quite different from its original headline licensing agreement with Agence France Presse a decade earlier.

A similar scenario played out in Australia, pitting both Google and Facebook against the Australian government in the form of the Australian Competition and Consumer Commission (ACCC). The issue of pushing the dominant digital platforms to negotiate equitable revenue-sharing agreements with Australian news sources did not involve

11 Directive (EU) 2019/790 of the European Parliament and of the Council of 17 April 2019 on copyright and related rights in the Digital Single Market and amending Directives 96/9/EC and 2001/29/EC; https:// eur-lex.europa.eu/eli/dir/2019/790/oj; accessed January 2, 2022.

12 "France's anti-trust authority fines Google €500 million in news copyright row," France24, July 13, 2021; https://www.france24.com /en/business/20210713-france-s-anti-trust-authority-fines-google- %E2%82%AC500-million-in-news-copyright-row; accessed January 2, 2022.

any changes to copyright legislation but instead was approached from the perspective of competition law. It was assumed that news providers had sufficient copyright in their content and photos, but the real issue was one of market dominance. Australia passed legislation giving the ACCC the authority to impose binding arbitration in cases where news providers and platforms could not agree on licensing terms for content. Despite strong pushback from both Google and Facebook, licensing agreements were secured with most relevant Australian media entities, and so far, the powers conferred on the ACCC by the legislation have not been used.

Canada is currently undertaking an approach similar to that of Australia,[13] passing legislation requiring negotiations between designated "digital news intermediaries" and "eligible news businesses" when the intermediaries make available news content on their services. "Making available" includes various forms of displaying content including snippets and links when applied to digital news intermediaries designated under the act. The legislation is being enacted even though some content-sharing agreements have been reached voluntarily between Google and several Canadian media outlets.

The news content issue was also reviewed by the U.S. Copyright Office to determine which approach, if any, should be taken by the U.S. to deal with the financial

---

13 Bill C-18, the "Online News Act"; https://www.parl.ca/legisinfo/en /bill/44-1/c-18; accessed November 3, 2022.

challenges facing traditional media. The study recognized that adequate funding for journalism may be at risk but concluded the "press publishers have significant protections under existing law and that the challenges of funding journalism in the internet era do not appear to be copyright-specific."[14] The issue of the use of news content by online platforms will no doubt continue to be a hot topic in many countries.

EDUCATIONAL COPYING IN CANADA

The advent of the photocopier in the 1950s, and subsequent improvements in copying technology, presented new challenges for authors and publishers. It became relatively simple and inexpensive to photocopy everything from books to newspaper clippings. Photocopying was particularly prevalent in the education sector, where textbooks were sometimes expensive or hard to come by, especially in less developed countries. I can remember when I lived in South Korea during the late 1980s, every university had several *poksa* copy shops located just outside the gates of the campus. They did a roaring business, taking apart books, copying them, and rebinding. It was quick and efficient. I will even confess that expatriates in Seoul resorted to the *poksa* to get sufficient copies of recent titles to discuss in their book discussion groups, as foreign books

14   U.S. Copyright Office, "Study on Ancillary Copyright Protections for Publishers," June 30, 2022; https://www.copyright.gov/policy/publishersprotections/; accessed November 3, 2022.

were rarely imported by booksellers and were costly to ship. There was no Amazon in those days and no e-books. Things have changed significantly in Korea since then. The availability of books in languages other than Korean has improved, and the country has strong copyright protection laws that are generally well enforced. *Poksa* shops still exist, but their role has changed, and they are now similar to printing outlets such as Staples or FedEx.

Even in developed countries, teachers and professors fell into the habit of photocopying materials from books for use by students. In universities, these were often sold as course packs; in elementary and secondary schools, they were often used as teaching aids. Fair dealing or fair use exceptions allowed limited unlicensed copying for purposes of research or private study, but the issue, then as now, was how much use was fair. Given the nature of the copying that was taking place within educational institutions, it was virtually impossible to verify either the extent or type of copying that was taking place. Copying that fell outside fair dealing criteria required permission from the copyright holder. How could individual teachers and professors in multiple schools and institutions secure permission when it was needed? In Canada, the solution was the establishment in the late 1980s of not-for-profit copyright collectives covering published materials, one for Québec, known as Copibec (originally the Union des écrivaines et écrivains Québécois) and one for English Canada, known originally by the name CanCopy, subsequently changed to Access Copyright.[15] The purpose of these collectives is primarily to represent authors and publishers (who make up the membership of the organizations) and to license the content of those members to users, at the same time offering a way to clear rights simply and efficiently. Canadian collectives have reciprocal arrangements with collecting societies in other countries, allowing the collection of royalties for Canadian authors in those countries and the collection of royalties for foreign authors in Canada. The collectives offer various forms of blanket and pay-as-you-go licences. Access Copyright currently (at time of publication) has affiliation agreements with approximately 700 publishers and 13,000 authors and bilateral agreements with collective management organizations in over thirty countries. Overall, the repertoire (inventory) consists of hundreds of millions of works.

In the case of educational institutions, given the widespread practice of photocopying for instructional use, licence agreements based on an agreed cost per student were signed in the early days of the collectives. The cost per student has varied over the years, depending on the level of education and the amount of presumed copying, but it generally ranged from a few dollars per year per student to twenty dollars or more. These funds were received

15 The full legal names for Copibec and Access Copyright are, respectively, la Société québécoise de gestion collective des droits de reproduction and the Canadian Copyright Licensing Agency.

by the collective and returned to authors and publishers, less administrative fees. The licence agreements gave the institutions the right to allow their personnel to widely copy materials held in the repertoire of the collectives for educational purposes, although the right to copy was not unlimited. Licences generally limited copying to 10 percent of a work for personal use, 15 percent if the copies were to be sold (such as in course packs), the whole of a chapter if it constituted 20 percent or less of a book, a short story, poem, or journal article from a book or periodical containing other works, or a newspaper article.[16] These ground rules were applied to digital copies as they came to replace photocopies. If there was disagreement over the royalty rate (or tariff) to be paid, the dispute was referred to the Copyright Board of Canada, a quasi-judicial tribunal established in 1989 to set tariffs based on a determination of the amount of copying taking place over a fixed period.

That was the situation that prevailed until about 2010, when some provincial educational authorities and institutions questioned the utility of paying the licence fees. They decided to withdraw from agreements with Access Copyright and Copibec and instead invoked fair dealing to justify their unlicensed use. A couple of key court decisions, beginning with CCH v Law Society of Upper Canada in

16 "Copying Right: A guide for Canada's universities to copyright, fair dealing and collective licensing," Association of Universities and Colleges of Canada (AUCC), August 2002; https://www.tru.ca/library/pdf /copyingright-e.pdf; accessed January 3, 2022.

2004[17] and then Alberta v Access Copyright in 2012,[18] had expanded the concept of fair dealing by placing a greater emphasis on users' rights, which the Supreme Court of Canada declared had to be given a "large and liberal interpretation."[19] In 2012, education was added as a fair dealing exception as part of changes to the Copyright Act, further opening the door to widespread unlicensed copying. In the postsecondary sector, Universities Canada, the umbrella group for most universities in Canada, developed

17   CCH Canadian Ltd. v Law Society of Upper Canada, 2004 SCC 13 (CanLII), [2004] 1 SCR 339; https://www.canlii.org/en/ca/scc/doc/2004/2004scc13/2004scc13.html; accessed January 4, 2022. In this case, the Law Society was accused of copyright infringement because it provided photocopying services of legal materials held in its collection to patrons; those who physically visited its library used (for a fee) photocopiers on the premises, or the Law Society staff made the copies and faxed them to users. The Society was sued by Canadian publishers of law-related publications. The case ultimately went to the Supreme Court, which ruled that the Society's practice of providing a single copy was a fair dealing on the basis that the works copied were for the purpose of research by users.

18   Alberta (Education) v Canadian Copyright Licensing Agency (Access Copyright), 2012 SCC 37; https://scc-csc.lexum.com/scc-csc/scc-csc/en/item/9997/index.do; accessed January 4, 2022. This decision of the Supreme Court reviewed, on appeal from the Federal Court of Appeal, a Copyright Board decision that had determined that photocopies of short excerpts from books made by teachers for students in elementary and secondary schools were subject to royalty payments. The court reversed the board's decision and remanded the question back to the board for further consideration on the basis that the teachers' activities fell within the fair dealing definitions of "research or private study."

19   In CCH v Law Society, the Supreme Court (para 48) declared that a fair dealing exception is a "user's right" and not simply a defence. It then stated (para 51) that "'(R)esearch' must be given a large and liberal interpretation in order to ensure that user's rights are not unduly constrained."

its own self-declared fair dealing guidelines. Under these guidelines, the limited copying that had previously been licensed from the collectives was declared to be a fair dealing, and many universities terminated their licence agreements. The stage was set for legal confrontation.

In 2013, licensing negotiations between York University and Access Copyright broke down. York refused to acquire a licence and refused to pay the per-student fee, even though the Copyright Board had, on an interim basis, certified a tariff that universities should pay per student in lieu of a licensing agreement when they used materials within the repertoire of the collective without a licence. The Copyright Board's tariff was considered mandatory in such cases. This was a form of legal backstop for the collective licensing process to ensure the functioning of the system. The alternative would be a requirement for individual authors to bring infringement lawsuits against individual institutions for individual cases of infringement, a practical impossibility. York's defence was that it was not required to obtain a licence or pay the tariff because any unlicensed copying done at the university was protected by fair dealing, as established by its published guidelines.

Access Copyright won the first round at the Federal Court in 2017, with the court ruling that not only was York required to pay the tariff but that its fair dealing guidelines were not fair because they permitted infringing uses. York appealed and partially prevailed, with the Federal Court of Appeal ruling that the so-called mandatory tariffs were, in fact, not mandatory for users like York. They were mandatory only to the extent that if York wished to acquire a licence and was refused, it could nonetheless pay the tariff and be protected from charges of infringement. In other words, they were mandatory for the licensing organization but not for the user.

In reaching its decision, the court went back to the 1930s and the origins of the collective licensing system, which at that time applied only to music performing rights organizations. The Court of Appeal did not, however, rule on York's fair dealing guidelines, stating there was no issue to try since the tariffs were not mandatory. In July 2021, the court's decision was upheld by the Supreme Court of Canada.[20] It now remains to be seen whether Parliament will amend the Copyright Act to clarify the role of collective licensing organizations.

The result of this prolonged litigation is that the collective licensing system for publishing in Canada has been rendered dysfunctional, and authors and publishers have been effectively prevented from being reimbursed for use of their work in educational settings. The result has been a collapse of the Canadian educational publishing market, leading inevitably over the long term to a significant reduction in the amount of Canadian material available for use in schools and universities. While the right of users to

20   York University v Canadian Copyright Licensing Agency (Access Copyright), 2021 scc 32, https://www.scc-csc.ca/case-dossier/cb/2021/39222-eng.aspx; accessed January 4, 2022.

access portions of works for specified purposes, including a socially beneficially purpose such as learning, has long been recognized, the combination of new technologies and liberal interpretations of fair dealing by the courts has significantly undermined the rights of authors and publishers in Canada to the benefit of the education industry.

In justifying their decision to avoid collective licensing, the universities have argued that they are helping to keep student costs down. Yet the institutions have not chosen to cut food costs in cafeterias or eliminate parking fees on campus. They have not even reduced student fees but instead have cut costs on the backs of authors. The result to date has been a colossal waste of public money by many of Canada's postsecondary institutions, who have chosen to incur large legal fees while hiring unnecessary staff, all to avoid paying a reasonable tariff to Canadian authors and publishers for reproducing their works in the teaching materials they provide to their students.

Universities Canada has reported that based on a survey it did of its member institutions between the fall of 2016 and the summer of 2017, Canadian universities, on average, had hired the equivalent of two additional full-time staff dedicated to copyright management since 2012.[21] Larger universities have hired more. While these figures were cited to demonstrate to the Supreme Court that

21 Richard C. Owens, "Universities should stop stealing copyright material," *National Post*, April 16, 2021; https://financialpost.com/opinion/richard-c-owens-universities-should-stop-stealing-copyright-material; accessed January 14, 2022.

member universities took the issue of respecting copyright seriously, they also demonstrate the unnecessary resources universities have dedicated to fighting the simple principle of licensing content for educational use. For example, there are seventy-seven universities outside Québec that have hired on average the equivalent of two additional full-time staff dedicated to copyright management since 2012.[22] These staff members presumably spend their time trying to ensure that university users are aware of and follow the institution's fair dealing policy as well as seeking to acquire copyright licenses when they are required. This adds up to a lot of personnel, totaling at least 154 new full-time positions since the universities decided not to licence content from Access Copyright.

Most of these costs could have been avoided by the simple expedient of securing a single licence or paying the tariff, since the university would have been granted a blanket licence to use content within the repertoire. One of the main functions of a copyright collective is to provide an efficient and effective mechanism for users to obtain permission to reproduce and use copyrighted works published by multiple copyright holders, savings and efficiencies that the universities have decided to forgo. It is impossible to know exactly how much the added costs of these 154 staff members amounted to, but a fair estimate would be about

22 After a prolonged dispute over licensing led by Laval University, Quebec's universities agreed to a content licensing agreement with Copibec in 2018.

$80,000 to $85,000 per full-time staff member in 2021, including benefits, which on average amount to 13 percent of staff costs. Thus, the cost for this additional copyright management staff amounted to approximately $12.5 to $13 million dollars annually, not including office overhead. How does this compare to the cost of paying the current Access Copyright tariff, which the Copyright Board has set at $14.31 per student? It is almost the same: $13 to $14 million annually. Rather than investing these largely public funds into the creation of more and better Canadian content through payment to authors and publishers, the universities have instead chosen to increase staffing levels.

For the most recent year for which figures are available from the Canadian Association of University Teachers, 2017–18, the total cost of university education in Canada was slightly more than $38 billion dollars. If divided by the most recent reported number of full-time equivalent university students in Canada (1,027,644), that amounts to a per capita cost of around $37,000. The tariff set by the Copyright Board amounts to less than .0004 percent of the average annual cost per student (or less than four cents a day). Universities proclaim from the rooftops that they are in favour of balanced copyright,[23] but their actions belie this claim. It is hard to understand the obstinacy and ideological positioning that has led the majority of Canadian universities into this position of opposing reasonable pay-

23 "Copyright and Fair Dealing," Universities Canada, https://www
.univcan.ca/priorities/copyright-and-fair-dealing/; accessed January 4, 2021.

ment to authors for using their content to teach the next generation of students.

SUMMARY

This chapter looks at various examples of unauthorized and unlicensed use in the U.S., Canada, and elsewhere. Some of these uses have been determined to fall within fair use or fair dealing, while others are still subject to litigation or potential legislation. Determining the exact line between a legal and an infringing unauthorized use is not always straightforward and can change over time. The current situation of the Canadian educational publication market has resulted from conflicting positions over the requirement to pay for access to copyrighted content, an unfortunate confrontation affecting authors, publishers, teachers, and educational institutions.

Disputes over whether certain unlicensed uses are legal or a modern version of book piracy reflect the ongoing tug-of-war between authors and publishers, who wish to exercise their right to control and monetize access to their content, and those who seek to build a business using that content without permission of the copyright holder. This applies to libraries exploiting unauthorized digital lending models and internet platforms free riding on the content of news providers.

Postsecondary institutions are also in business — the education business. They compete for students based on the excellence of their product, the fees that they charge, and the physical and social environment they offer. As businesses, they have a responsibility to pay fairly for the inputs that they use, whether these are salaries, infrastructure costs, or academic materials. The stretching of the rights of students by most of Canada's post-secondary institutions outside Québec to unfairly exploit the copyrighted works of others is an inexcusable business and moral lapse.

CHAPTER 7

Contemporary Copyright Challenges: Artificial Intelligence, Blockchain, and Traditional Cultural Expression

CHANGING TECHNOLOGY HAS always presented challenges to existing business models, and copyright is no exception. While new means of producing content — such as photography, sound recordings in various formats (ranging from wax cylinders to vinyl records, from cassette tapes to MP3 files), motion pictures, television, content on tapes and discs, and now online streaming, video games, and e-books — have required regular updating of copyright laws, the basic principles protecting the rights of authors to exploit their work, while allowing for limited exceptions, have not changed. Alongside the emergence of new forms of content have come new forms of reproduction, many of them used by content pirates. Just about any technology can be used for both legitimate and illegitimate ends. Copyright holders have responded with new technologies such as technological protection measures (TPMs) that are designed to limit access to and reproduction of digital content.

TPMs enable many of the digital distribution models existing today, as they allow copyright holders to provide differentiated access in return for differentiated degrees of payment. Thus, digital files can be made available for one or more users for varying periods of time, depending on the terms of the licence. To do this, TPMs control both access (allowing users to view the content) and copying (restricting the ability to reproduce it). Both are required to make the digital business model work, and it is this business model that allows creative industries to develop and bring new content to users. Copyright holders have also been successful in ensuring that copyright law has evolved to account for new technologies, for example by restricting the circumvention of TPMs through international instruments such as the WIPO Copyright Treaty.

There are those who argue that it should be legal to circumvent access controls in order to exercise fair dealing or fair use rights. This misunderstands the nature of a digital work. In terms of access controls, arguing that it is legitimate to break into TPM-protected digital content to make a reproduction that might fall within the definition of fair use or fair dealing is like arguing that it is okay to steal a newspaper from the newsstand in order to make an unlicensed but non-infringing photocopy of an article for purposes of research or private study. Regarding copy controls, in Canadian law there is no explicit provision preventing the circumvention of copying (described in law as "controls to protect the exclusive rights of copyright owners"), but the technological reality is that access and content controls are generally one and the same. There are, however, some exceptions in the law for practical reasons: law enforcement and national security; reverse engineering for software compatibility; encryption research; verification as to whether a TPM permits the collection or communication of personal information; security testing of computer systems; accessibility for disabled persons; temporary recordings made by broadcasters for technical reasons; and unlocking cell phones.[1] Under these limited circumstances, circumvention is legal.

ARTIFICIAL INTELLIGENCE

Technology will continue to evolve, and copyright will continue to need to adapt. One of the major new challenges facing the copyright world is artificial intelligence and AI's prime mechanism, algorithms. To what extent can copyright be associated with content created by machines, and will machine-generated content come to replace human creation in many areas? This is a question currently under

---

1 Brian P. Isaac and Brian Chau, "Circumvention of Technological Protection Measures (TPMs) prohibited," Smart & Biggar, December 5, 2012; https://www.smartbiggar.ca/insights/publication/circumvention-of -technological-protection-measures-(tpms)-prohibited#:~:text=TPMs%20 are%20defined%20in%20the,such%20as%20copying%20the%20work; accessed February 4, 2022.

consideration in many countries. The intrusion of artificial intelligence into our daily lives has raised major questions of ethics among researchers, companies that are developing and using AI, and, of course, consumers. Already, algorithms play an important if largely invisible role in our daily affairs, controlling everything from how our tax returns are assessed to the ads that we receive online to our insurability and calculation of life expectancy.

There are many definitions of AI, but essentially it involves allowing machines to assess and interpret data and then make decisions that in the past would have been made by humans. Human intelligence is based on reasoning informed by past experiences, education, context, and sometimes emotion. AI can replicate some of these inputs very effectively. Algorithms fuel the machine learning process so that true AI goes beyond just interpreting data. It allows the machine to learn from the data (discerning patterns) and in so doing improves its prediction and problem-solving capacities, sometimes even allowing it to create something entirely new. How does all this affect ethics and, more specifically, copyright?

The creation by AI of a work of art, a piece of music, or a written work potentially subject to copyright protection has already happened, raising the question of how to deal with such works. If only humans are capable of creating works that are subject to copyright protection, then how does one deal with works produced by a seemingly autonomous machine? The U.S. Copyright Office provides some guidance on AI-created works, noting that it will not register works "produced by a machine or mere mechanical process that operates randomly or automatically without any creative input or intervention from a human author." But what about a machine that allows people to compose music (even though they don't have the ability to read or write music) by manipulating various musical elements, such as rhythm, harmonics, etc., to blend them into a new piece of music? They exist! How much human creativity is involved? Not much, so is the end product a creation of the software or of the human enabled by the software?

We already have the example of photography, where human involvement in many cases seems to be decreasing. Initially, photography was thought to be an entirely mechanical process, devoid of creativity. Today, most people would not agree, and photographs have been protected under copyright in most countries for many years. But as machines have progressed, there is less and less artistic creativity required to take a photograph, although one could argue that human involvement is required more than ever to take a *good* photograph. Nonetheless, today smartphone technology is so advanced that all that is required to take a passable photograph is a reasonable eye for composition and light. The device makes almost all the technical decisions, and in some cases, it even clicks its own shutter. Yet photographs, or at least most photographs, are protected by copyright.

The key issue is creative input or originality. If the work is of a mechanical or manual nature where another author would have arrived at essentially the same outcome following the same process, that is indicative of a lack of originality, and the work is not protectable.[2] This raises the question of whether a computer can make a creative choice.

Remember the monkey selfie case discussed in Chapter 3? Partly as a result of that case, the U.S. Copyright Office clarified that for a work to be protected by copyright, it had to be created by a human.[3] It also dismissed a claim by a Dr. Stephen Thaler to register a computer-generated work of art that was the output of Thaler's AI system known as the Creativity Machine.[4] (Thaler launched a court appeal.) While to date neither an animal nor a machine can create a copyrighted work (at least not in the U.S.), does this mean that the human who created the work by making all the creative choices behind taking the photograph or programming the computer is the author? What if a human creates a robot that takes photographs, writes a work of fiction, or

---

2 Gervais, p. 105.

3 Compendium of U.S. Copyright Office Practices, U.S. Copyright Office, Chapter 300, Subsection 306, 3d ed, 2021; https://www.copyright .gov/comp3/; accessed January 7, 2022.

4 Franklin Graves, "Thaler Pursues Copyright Challenge Over Denial of AI-Generated Work Registration," *IP Watchdog*, June 6, 2022; https:// ipwatchdog.com/2022/06/06/thaler-pursues-copyright-challenge -denial-ai-generated-work-registration/id=149463/; accessed November 3, 2022.

produces a painting? Can the work be copyrighted by the creator behind the robot's programming?

This is not a hypothetical question. Sony has developed software capable of composing music. Is the robot the instrument of the creator, in the same way that a graphic design tool or software in the hands of its creator is the instrument that fixes the creation, or, if the robot has artificial intelligence capabilities, is the robot the creator? If so, this would seem to put all machine-produced works into the public domain, with no economic return to or incentive for the creator. This would not only discourage the development of AI but also handicap creators.

What if the human behind the technology is considered the author? This opens other challenges. Could works created by artists using AI technology be considered joint works (that is, shared between the artist and the creator of the AI program) if the result is a product that goes beyond the creative expectations of the original artist? What happens if there are multiple creators, for example, a software programmer, a technician who manipulates the program to create a new work (such as a computer-generated image), and perhaps even the company owning the proprietary software? This would be a nightmare for companies seeking to license the end product, not knowing who has the copyright. Given the potential for confusion, sticking to basic principles of creativity and ownership is important.

In determining who should hold the copyright to a work produced by a computer program, there are a couple of schools of thought. One is to confer the copyright on the software programmer, or perhaps to share the copyright between the software programmer and the artist manipulating or operating the program. Another is to take the position that even with a software program, there is no creation without human intervention, so the copyright should go to the artist using the program, in the same way that an author claims the ownership of a book written on a laptop, not the producer of the software or hardware that makes the laptop function. Under this interpretation, there is always human judgment involved in directing the program, making choices, accepting outputs, etc., much in the same way that a film director creates an audiovisual work. These are the kinds of issues that courts and legislators are beginning to address.

Infringement is another important issue that needs to be addressed if AI-generated works are denied copyright protection. What happens when there is unauthorized reproduction of an AI-created work? If there is no copyright, there is no infringement. A Chinese court recently dealt with this issue,[5] finding that an automated article written by a program called Dreamwriter (created by Tencent), which had been copied and published without permission by another Chinese company, Yinxun, was nevertheless subject to copyright protection because it met the origi-

5 "Court rules AI-written article has copyright," *China Daily Global*, January 9, 2020; http://www.ecns.cn/news/2020-01-09/detail -ifzsqcrm6562963.shtml; accessed January 7, 2022.

nality test through the involvement of a creative group of editors. These people performed several functions to direct the program, such as arranging the data input and format, selecting templates for the structure of the article, and training the algorithm model. In other words, there was sufficient human authorship, and thus there was copyright and therefore infringement of copyright. Remember that in addition to human attribution, the work must also be sufficiently original and not just a list or compilation of facts.

There is a further infringement scenario to consider. What if a computer-generated program is itself responsible for the infringement? After all, artificially created content is based on the program being fed examples of original content so that the algorithm can learn the patterns that go into content creation. In this scenario, if there is no human creator, who is liable for the infringement? This demonstrates why there needs to be human attribution in the process.

Yet another issue related to AI and copyright is the use of copyrighted material to train automated systems. For example, if a machine is to be trained to write a romance novel, it must be fed numerous romance novel models to be able to understand the basic premise and structure. This raises issues over the appropriate use of copyrighted material as well as broader ethical issues of whether it is acceptable to ingest another's work without consent just because it is efficient. Some countries already have fair dealing exceptions that allow some data mining within set limits, such as research for non-commercial purposes. (Canada has this issue under review.) In the case of the U.S., there is a fair use structure that can be used to adjudicate the acceptability of data mining within established parameters, but the use of data mining to create new AI-generated works is particularly problematic for copyright holders and may not be a fair use. The issue has not yet been tested in a U.S. court although it soon will be as there are already cases before the judiciary.[6]

The most recent example of widespread unauthorized data scraping is AI-generated art created with text prompts through platforms such as DALL-E, Midjourney, or Stability.AI's Stable Diffusion. A prompt might be "Toronto skyline at sunset in the style of Monet." The platform will produce several works for the user based on millions of data points that it has accessed, normally images scraped off art and photography sites on the internet. Many of the images will be in the public domain — like all of Monet's works — but many others will be works under copyright, especially if the user requests that the work be done in the style of a living artist or an artist or photographer whose work is still under copyright. The question of AI-generated art has now been transposed to the world of written content with the emergence of AI tools such as ChatGPT,

6   James Vincent, "Getty Images sues AI art generator Stable Diffusion in the U.S. for copyright infringement," The Verge, February 26, 2023; https://www.theverge.com/2023/2/6/23587393/ai-art-copyright-lawsuit -getty-images-stable-diffusion; accessed March 25, 2023

which, like the models that produce images based on unlicensed inputs, generates text based on scraping material found on the internet such as news reports, novels, poems, research articles, and other publications, all without any authorization from the copyright holders.

Apart from the issue of permission, there is the very real concern that AI-generated work might compete with or substitute for the original. While some artists, designers, illustrators, and writers are incorporating AI into their work, for others there is the possibility that they will be made redundant by the output of an algorithm. The most bitter pill is that the algorithm is likely being fed copyrighted work without any payment to the artist or author in order to produce a work that might put them out of business. Building a business model on the back of content owned by others is an issue that is being tested in court, because licensing of content for research and data mining is a revenue stream that copyright holders can legitimately exploit. The tech industry justifies this in the name of innovation. Governments eager to climb on the AI bandwagon have contemplated instituting wide text and data mining exceptions that would destroy licensing models. At the same time, it is worth remembering that without human creation, without artists and authors, there would be no AI. To deny authors the right to consent to the use of their work is, to my mind, unethical, immoral, and, in the end, self-defeating. As Canada considers its position on this topic — as it is currently doing through a consultation paper on copyright, artificial intelligence, and the "Internet of Things"[7] — it will be important not to throw copyright and all its economic and cultural benefits under the bus. Governments and the World Intellectual Property Organization[8] are actively considering how to define authorship in the case of AI-generated works. Finding a way to entrench human creativity into the AI framework will continue to be an important task to preserve the relevance of copyright.

BLOCKCHAIN TECHNOLOGY AND NFTS (NON-FUNGIBLE TOKENS)

What is blockchain technology and how does it relate to copyright? Blockchain is best known for its role in underpinning digital currency, such as Bitcoin. There are many explanations of how the blockchain works, but one I thought described it succinctly was provided by Klaus Schwab, founder and executive chairman of the World Economic Forum, in his book *The Fourth Industrial Revolution*: "In essence, the blockchain is a shared, programmable, cryptographically secure and therefore trusted ledger which no

7 Government of Canada, "A Consultation on a Modern Copyright Framework for Artificial Intelligence and the Internet of Things", July 16, 2021; https://ised-isde.canada.ca/site/strategic-policy-sector/en/market-place-framework-policy/copyright-policy/consultation-modern-copyright-framework-artificial-intelligence-and-internet-things-0; accessed March 28, 2023.

8 "Artificial Intelligence and Intellectual Property," World Intellectual Property Organization, Geneva; https://www.wipo.int/about-ip/en/frontier_technologies/ai_and_ip.html; accessed January 7, 2022.

single user controls and which can be inspected by anyone."[9] Blocks are unique numbers designating a single use or work, chained together and verifiable by anyone in the chain. Blockchains are decentralized, borderless, censorship-resistant, tamper-proof, and universal. One copyright application that has been suggested for blockchain is to set up a global registry of authors to serve as a medium for licensing. The World Economic Forum has identified five new functions in an artist-centric model for blockchain:

1. enabling smart contracts, which will help provide fairer terms for artists;
2. establishing transparent P2P transactions that would reveal who accessed the work and how much revenue it is generating at any given time;
3. promoting efficient, dynamic pricing by recording who has been granted access to a work so pricing can be adjusted;
4. allowing micro-monetizing, for example by charging for song snippets; and
5. establishing a reputation system that would promote cooperation and record and reveal bad behaviour.[10]

9 Ryo Takahashi, "How can creative industries benefit from block-chain?" World Economic Forum, July 18, 2017, quoting Klaus Schwab, *The Fourth Industrial Revolution*, Crown Business, New York, 2016; https://www.weforum.org/agenda/2017/07/how-can-creative-industries -benefit-from-blockchain/; accessed February 5, 2022.

10 Takahashi.

The Alliance of Independent Authors,[11] a global non-profit for self-publishing authors, has also proposed that blockchain could help self-published authors by enabling them to be in direct contact with consumers, thus bypassing publishers (as is already done with self-publishing) and online distributors (which is not). The Canadian copyright collective Access Copyright, in conjunction with several visual arts collectives, is developing a blockchain-based ledger to ascertain provenance for visual arts, offering Canadian visual artists a place to register their work and link content to its creators so that artists receive appropriate credit and financial compensation. The initial work is being funded in part by a $495,000 grant from the Canada Council for the Arts.[12]

But if blockchain offers opportunities for copyright by allowing copyright holders to exercise greater control over the distribution of their work, it also poses significant challenges, particularly with respect to non-fungible tokens, known as NFTs.

As is the case with blockchain, there are many definitions of NFTs available, but I like this one:

---

11 Orna Ross, "Authors and Blockchain," Alliance of Independent Authors, London, September 4, 2017; https://selfpublishingadvice.org/authors-and-blockchain/; accessed February 5, 2022.

12 Porter Anderson, "Prescient Innovations Blockchain Lab Gains Canada Council Funding," *Publishing Perspectives*, July 10, 2019; https://publishingperspectives.com/2019/07/access-copyright-prescient-innovations-blockchain-lab-gains-canada-council-funding/; accessed February 5, 2022.

NFTS are digital certificates that authenticate a claim of ownership to an asset and allow it to be transferred or sold. The certificates are secured with blockchain technology similar to what underpins Bitcoin and other cryptocurrencies ... [Unlike Bitcoin] NFTS are by definition non-fungible [cannot be substituted], and thus, are deployed as individual chains of ownership to track a specific asset.... NFTS are designed to uniquely restrict and represent a unique claim on an asset.[13]

That is precisely where things get weird. Often, NFTS are used to claim "ownership" of a digital asset that is otherwise completely copiable, pasteable and shareable, such as a movie, JPEG, or other digital file.

NFTS exist only digitally, but, unlike most digital images, they cannot be duplicated as each has a unique digital signature (although a semblance of the NFT can certainly be reproduced). Basketball fans can buy unique NFTS of video highlights of NBA games, a collectible that can be traded or sold, even though the same clip can be viewed for free on YouTube. But the NFT owned by the fan is identified and unique. I guess it is a bit like anyone being able to see Monet's *The Artist's Garden at Giverny* in an art magazine or even on the internet, but the one and only original is in the Musée d'Orsay in Paris.

13 Luke Heemsbergen, "NFTs Explained: What They Are & Why They Are Selling for Millions," The Fashion Law, March 11, 2021; https://www.thefashionlaw.com/nfts-explained-what-they-are-and-why-they-are-selling-for-millions-of-dollars/; accessed February 5, 2022.

An NFT can be made out of just about anything digital — images, text, videos, music, etc. — and just like the famous Dutch tulip bulb, it is a product of scarcity. It has value because someone will pay something for it, expecting that in the future it can be sold to someone else who will be willing to pay even more for it.

With respect to the copyright in the images on which the NFT is based, it is the creator of the artwork or music in an NFT who owns the copyright to the underlying work, not the purchaser of the token unless the sale includes the sale of certain rights. In many cases, even though the buyer is the sole owner of a particular NFT, the artist who created the work to which the NFT is linked could continue to produce copies of the work. This sets up the possibility that NFTs of a work could be sold without the creator's permission, or even their knowledge. Artists have found their work appropriated by sellers of NFTs without permission. It's like finding your artwork adorning posters and T-shirts being sold on the internet without permission or licensing. In effect, images and music are being pirated by anonymous users minting NFTs based on artists' work without their permission. Just as so often occurs with new technology, NFTs are a double-edged sword. They offer the potential of a new revenue stream for some artists, but they also open a Pandora's box of new forms of digital piracy.

TRADITIONAL CULTURAL EXPRESSIONS
Quite separate from AI and blockchain, but also a challenge to traditional concepts of copyright as they have

evolved over the past three hundred years, is the issue of traditional or Indigenous cultural expression. Historically, copyright has been embedded in the western concept of individual creation and expression. It affords protection to the author for a finite period, and while there is provision in copyright law for joint authorship and even different rights for individual copyright holders within a group work such as a film production, it does not lend itself well to communal creation or to the protection of traditional art forms in perpetuity. This is often the form taken by a variety of traditional cultural expressions, such as music, dance, and visual art traditions. At the same time, it is important that Indigenous authors not be denied the benefits of copyright protection when they practice their traditional arts.

The World Intellectual Property Organization has been working on this issue for many years. Its website notes, "The current international system for protecting intellectual property was fashioned during the age of industrialization in the West and developed subsequently in line with the perceived needs of technologically advanced societies. However, in recent years, Indigenous peoples, local communities, and governments, mainly in developing countries, have demanded equivalent protection for traditional knowledge systems."[14]

14 "Traditional Knowledge and Intellectual Property — Background Brief," World Intellectual Property Organization, Geneva; https://www .wipo.int/pressroom/en/documents/background_brief_tk.pdf; accessed January 7, 2022.

It continues: "Recognizing traditional forms of creativity and innovation as protectable intellectual property would be an historic shift in international law, enabling Indigenous and local communities as well as governments to have a say over the use of their traditional knowledge by others. This would make it possible, for example, to protect traditional remedies and Indigenous art and music against misappropriation and enable communities to control and benefit collectively from their commercial exploitation."

The fact that no international agreement on how to protect traditional cultural expressions has yet emerged reflects the difficult issues needing to be resolved in many areas of creativity, music being but one example. In many countries (but certainly not all), music requires some form of fixation to be protected by copyright. In these jurisdictions, proving fixation for traditional music and performances can be problematic.

Traditional or Indigenous cultural expression is normally based on collective and communal ownership rather than ownership by any individual or small group of individuals. As such, there is no identified creator to whom the copyright can belong. Additionally, Indigenous culture is deeply imbued with the concept of stewardship as opposed to ownership. The dictionary definition of stewardship is "the conducting, supervising, or managing of something, especially the careful and responsible management of something entrusted to one's care." In the case of Indigenous cultural expression manifested through artifacts, songs, dances, and legends, stewardship can arise from family, clan, and spiritual responsibilities or beliefs. Individuals entrusted by their community and cultural traditions to exercise these responsibilities have the obligation to protect cultural expressions from misuse. As an example, an Indigenous design holding deep spiritual significance should not be used to decorate a doormat or a dish towel that is sold for commercial gain.

Adding a further dimension to this issue is the United Nations Declaration on the Rights of Indigenous Peoples (UNDRIP),[15] a document that Canada has embraced through legislation[16] requiring that Canadian federal laws be brought into conformity with the declaration. UNDRIP covers much more than culture when dealing with Indigenous rights, but it includes two articles relevant to Indigenous culture. Article 11 states, "Indigenous people have the right to practice and revitalize their cultural traditional customs. This includes the right to maintain, protect and develop the past, present and future manifestations of these cultures, such as archeological and historical sites, artefacts [sic], designs, ceremonies, technologies and visual

15 "United Nations Declaration on the Rights of Indigenous Peoples," (A/RES/61/295), United Nations, New York, September 13, 2007; https://www.un.org/development/desa/indigenouspeoples/declaration-on-the-rights-of-indigenous-peoples.html; accessed January 9, 2022.

16 "United Nations Declaration on the Rights of Indigenous Peoples Act," (S.C. 2021, c. 14), June 21, 2021; https://laws-lois.justice.gc.ca/eng/acts/U-2.2/; accessed January 9, 2022.

and performing arts and literature."[17]

This is supplemented by Article 31, which repeats the right to maintain, control, protect, and develop cultural heritage including literature, designs, visual and performing arts, and other aspects of traditional knowledge, and adds that Indigenous people enjoy the same rights with respect to the intellectual property attached to this heritage. Moreover, in conjunction with Indigenous peoples, states are required to take effective measures to recognize and protect these cultural rights.

In 2019, a parliamentary committee reviewing the Copyright Act[18] recognized the difficulty of dealing with Indigenous cultural expression within the parameters of the legislation. It commented: "The Committee recognizes that, in many cases, the Act fails to meet the expectations of Indigenous peoples with respect to the protection, preservation, and dissemination of their cultural expressions. The Committee also recognizes the need to effectively protect traditional arts and cultural expressions in a manner that empowers Indigenous communities, and to ensure that individual Indigenous creators have the same opportunities to fully participate in the Canadian economy as

17 UNDRIP; https://www.un.org/development/desa/indigenouspeoples/
wp-content/uploads/sites/19/2018/11/UNDRIP_E_web.pdf; accessed
January 9, 2022.

18 "Statutory Review of the Copyright Act," INDU Committee, May 16,
2019; https://www.ourcommons.ca/Committees/en/INDU/StudyActivity
?studyActivityId=9897131; accessed January 9, 2022.

non-Indigenous creators."[19]

Among its recommendations[20] were the participation of Indigenous groups in the development of national and international intellectual property law, the creation of an Indigenous art registry, and granting Indigenous peoples the authority to manage traditional arts and cultural expressions through the insertion of a non-derogation clause in the Copyright Act. This would subordinate protections under the act to Indigenous constitutional and treaty rights.

Consultation and participation are desirable, but what it will lead to is an open question. Will there be two legal systems to protect creativity, one designed for traditional arts and cultural expressions and another for everything else? This raises the immediate question of what constitutes traditional arts and whether Indigenous groups have the sole right to use those arts. Are non-Indigenous creators prevented from drawing on existing traditional art forms to create new expressions? Assuming traditional knowledge is defined in a way that achieves broad agreement and is then fenced off, a question that quickly arises is, "Who gets to claim it?"

In the U.S., the Indian Arts and Crafts Act of 1990[21]

---

19 INDU Committee, Indigenous Matter, p.87ff; https://www.ourcommons .ca/DocumentViewer/en/42-1/INDU/report-16/page-87#15; accessed January 9, 2022.

20 INDU Committee, Recommendation 5.

21 The Indian Arts and Crafts Act of 1990, U.S. Department of the Interior, https://www.doi.gov/iacb/act; accessed January 9, 2022.

prohibits "non-Indians" from offering for sale in the U.S. any product that falsely suggests it is Indian-produced. The legislation defines who is recognized as "Indian," but whenever anyone defines who is included, at the same time they define who is excluded. What about individuals who identify as Indigenous and who are recognized as such by one or more Indigenous communities or nations, but who may not meet the legal definition? This becomes a real issue when it comes to accusations of cultural appropriation. There is a delicate balancing act between protecting Indigenous rights to cultural expression and exercising control over who gets to access that culture.

While the copyright slipper does not seem to fit the foot of Native culture very well, there have nonetheless been some instances where copyright has played a role in protecting native art and designs and resolving disputes. There are several prominent cases in Australia, including one where the issue of group ownership of traditional cultural designs came into play in a copyright dispute involving the infringement of an Aboriginal artist's copyright on a painting.[22] The courts have recognized that traditional Aboriginal artworks fall under protection of the Copyright Act and that individual artists have an obligation to their community to prevent inappropriate uses of cultural symbols. Nonetheless, the principle is maintained that the

---

22 The Bulun Bulun Case: John Bulun Bulun & Anor v R & T Textiles Pty Ltd [1998] IndigLawB 87; (1998) 4(16) Indigenous Law Bulletin 24; http://www8.austlii.edu.au/cgi-bin/viewdoc/au/journals/IndigLawB/1998/87.html; accessed January 9, 2022.

copyright still belongs to an individual creator even if the work of that creator is based on pre-existing traditional communal symbols.

Strengthening copyright law in Canada by adding an artists' resale right would also help Indigenous artists. Many of them sold their original works for a pittance, yet as their work gained fame and value, they could only try to capture that value by producing subsequent works. The most famous example of this injustice is the work of Kenojuaq Ashevak, the Inuit artist who created the work *Enchanted Owl*, featured, among other places, on a Canadian postage stamp. Kenojuaq, who was from Cape Dorset where the famous Arctic art co-operative was founded in the 1970s, is no longer alive. She died in 2013 at the age of eighty-five. In November 2018, the original of *Enchanted Owl* sold for $216,000, a Canadian record for work by an Inuit artist. It had previously sold in 2001 for $58,650. Kenojuaq first sold the work in 1960 for $24, and neither she nor her estate has received a penny from the resales of the original work. The Nunavut Arts and Crafts Association has been actively advocating for the incorporation of a resale right in Canadian copyright law.[23]

Copyright law will have to adapt to accommodate some of the requirements needed to protect traditional Indigenous

23 Kent Driscoll, "Canadian arts organization pushing feds to amend copyright act after sale of Inuit painting The Enchanted Owl," APTN National News, November 29, 2018; https://www.aptnnews.ca/national -news/canadian-arts-organization-pushing-feds-to-amend-copyright-act -after-sale-of-inuit-painting-the-enchanted-owl/; accessed January 9, 2022.

cultural expressions — or a parallel system of protection will need to be devised. The intersection of different forms of protection for cultural creations will, however, present challenges, particularly where the foundations of western copyright law and those of Indigenous cultural expression and stewardship are not in harmony. Would a work that is sacred to Indigenous people yet lies in the public domain be commercially exploitable, for example as a logo on a T-shirt? These are questions that copyright practitioners, legislators and officials, and organizations like WIPO need to deal with now and in the future.

SUMMARY

Copyright has adapted many times over the centuries to meet challenges imposed by changing technology, and this will continue, particularly given the role of artificial intelligence. If there is no human attribution to works created through AI and no human responsibility attached to the tools used by AI, such as algorithms, the foundations of copyright will be severely tested. Blockchain technology offers the possibility of creating an unbroken link between artist and work but can also lend itself to new forms of digital piracy, as is happening today with NFTs. These challenges, along with the limited ability of copyright to address questions arising from the need to protect traditional Indigenous cultural expressions, are major issues facing practitioners of copyright in the twenty-first century.

CHAPTER 8

In Defence of Copyright

WE HAVE SEEN that copyright is a bundle of legal rights accorded to authors, the term used to describe creators across the broad spectrum of artistic and creative endeavours and industries. Copyright has been developed over the past three hundred years, drawing on both a utilitarian, economic rationale rooted in common law and a moral, property rights argument based on continental civil law traditions. It has expanded from limited geographical coverage confined to specific jurisdictions to become an internationally accepted and regulated regime, governed by treaty and incorporating international dispute settlement practices. As technology has changed, copyright law has adapted. From the outset, it was limited in terms of its duration, and, over the years, derogations and exceptions have been formulated to provide a range of specified uses not licensed by copyright holders. Its current challenges arise from new technologies, such as artificial intelligence and blockchain, and from very liberal court interpretations regarding fair dealing and fair use that have eroded traditional protections for authors.

In the Canadian context, these court interpretations have undermined much of the economic incentive for authors and publishers to produce materials for the elementary, secondary, and postsecondary education sectors, as we saw in Chapter 6. One of the principal reasons for providing protection to authors is to encourage production of new works. As the Statute of Anne put it, "for the encouragement of learning." While fair dealing (or fair use in the U.S.) exists to provide a balance, allowing limited access to an author's works without permission to promote learning and to facilitate functions such as literary criticism or news reporting, it has, in Canada in particular, gone too far. There has been steady expansion both in terms of court interpretation and additional statutory exceptions.

Limited exceptions for literary criticism or news reporting make sense because requiring permission for such uses would put manacles on these necessary functions, but over the years, other exceptions such as private study and research have been expanded. Since the early 2000s, through several key rulings, the Supreme Court of Canada has led the way in punching ever wider holes in authors' protection.[1] Added to these rulings was the ill-conceived and overly broad exception for education included in the

---

1 For example, CCH Canadian Ltd. v Law Society of Upper Canada, cited in Chapter 6, note 113, and Alberta (Education) v Canadian Copyright Licensing Agency (Access Copyright), Chapter 6, note 114.

Copyright Act in 2012. The impact on authors and the publishing industry has been highly damaging and has led to a direct reduction in educational publishing in Canada.

While it is entirely reasonable to allow students to access excerpts of copyrighted material without needing to secure a licence, which would be almost impossible for them to do, it is not unreasonable to expect that the institutions that provide educational materials (and which, in the post-secondary context, charge students for these materials) should obtain licences from copyright holders when they reproduce or aggregate content, such as in course packs or by photocopying or digitally reproducing content. Until recently, that process was facilitated through collective licensing, with Access Copyright and Copibec providing one-stop shops. Recent court rulings have pulled the legs out from under that system,[2] leaving no recourse but further litigation or legislative changes. While the education exception is unlikely to be removed, it should be limited so that it applies to teaching institutions only when licensed copies of works are not commercially available.

Robust copyright protection is essential for any country that wants to encourage innovation and promote cultural sovereignty. Copyright-related industries, such as publishing, filmmaking, music, video game production, software development, and other creative activities can only thrive

---

2 York University v Canadian Copyright Licensing Agency (Access Copyright); 2021 scc 32, July, 30, 2021; https://www.scc-csc.ca/case-dossier/cb/2021/39222-eng.aspx; accessed January 17, 2022.

if the essence of what is produced — the creative intellectual property — is protected as an incentive and as a reward. We saw in Chapter 4 how piracy saps the strength of copyright industries and undermines creativity and artistic production. It diverts billions of dollars away from authors and creative industries. We also saw how much is contributed by copyright industries to economic output. In Canada, that figure is over 3 percent of GDP; in the U.S., it is more than double that number. It is not a coincidence that the United States takes the protection of intellectual property more seriously and gives it a higher priority than governments have traditionally done in Canada.

While the economic argument for copyright protection is important, we should not lose sight of cultural sovereignty and equity arguments. If a country values its literary tradition, its history, its music, its art, and its ability to create and distribute stories through audiovisual means, it will honour and respect copyright. The weakening of the Canadian educational publishing market described above will reduce the amount of local content produced for Canadian schoolchildren. In the nineteenth century, the limited copyright protection afforded to foreign works in the United States encouraged U.S. publishers to pirate British works rather than invest in U.S. literature. Noted American historian Arthur M. Schlesinger wrote, "So long as publishers [...] could reprint, or pirate, popular English authors without payment of royalty, and so long as readers could buy such volumes far cheaper than books written by Americans, native authorship remained at a marked disadvantage."[3] Canada has produced a robust literary output in recent years, but most writers continue to struggle economically. Weakening copyright protection and taking ineffective action against piracy does nothing to encourage writers, artists, musicians, filmmakers, or any other creators to invest the time, effort, and money to continue to bring into existence new works that reflect local perspectives.

Copyright also has an important role to play in promoting equity and diversity. Copyright is blind to factors of race or gender. Once a work has been created, as long as it meets the established criteria (originality, fixation, and authorship), it is granted copyright protection automatically, assuming the creator is a resident of a Berne Convention country. An artist in Zaire, an author in Cuba, a composer in Greenland — they all qualify. I would argue that copyright is the ultimate enabler of democratic economic and moral rights because the simple act of creation confers the right. Unlike other forms of intellectual property, important as they are, copyright requires no formal process of registration. For example, it can be argued (and no doubt proved) that racialized or marginalized groups are underrepresented in the patent filing process because of barriers to filing (the process, cost, access to the system, and so on). There are no such overt barriers with copyright.

3 Arthur M. Schlesinger, *The Rise of the City, 1878–1898*, New York, MacMillan, 1933, p. 252.

Nonetheless, it could be argued that practices that follow from copyright are not necessarily free of bias. It is not difficult to find examples where the application of copyright in various business situations can be argued to be discriminatory, such as in reaching contractual agreements where one side may have disproportionate power. It is worth noting, however, that power imbalance in negotiations over payment for use of copyrighted material (e.g., an author with a publisher or a musician with a label) can and does happen quite frequently, independent of any racial considerations. Nevertheless, I think there is a view that while copyright may be race or gender neutral, its application is not always so. At the same time, it has historically been an instrument of empowerment. Two examples of this are Phillis Wheatley and Frederick Douglass.

An obvious example of the historical context of copyright was its application to slaves in a slave-owning society, such as the southern American states prior to the Emancipation Proclamation. Individual creators could hardly expect to avail themselves of their copyrights when they themselves were treated as chattel to be bought and sold. The earliest example of African-American literature, the poems of Phillis Wheatley, a slave girl in Massachusetts, published in 1773, illustrate the struggle faced by people of colour in trying to establish authorship. Wheatley had to appear before a group of notables (all white males, of course, no doubt of a certain age) who eventually established that the poetry had been produced by her, an authorship hurdle not known to have been forced on any other writer. Yet copyright prevailed in the end. The publication of her work was entered in Stationers' Hall, London, the repository for copyrighted works at the time (since the publication predated U.S. copyright and the U.S. Constitution), although it was undoubtedly the British publisher, Archibald Bell of Aldgate, who ensured it was deposited.

Another famous work of African-American literature, Frederick Douglass's *Narrative of the Life of Frederick Douglass, An American Slave* (1845) and a later work, *My Bondage, My Freedom* (1855), both bear an inscription on the flyleaf: "Entered, according to Act of Congress, in the year 1845 [or 1855] by Frederick Douglass, in the Clerk's office of the District Court of...." (It was Massachusetts for the first work and the Northern District of New York for the second.) Prior to 1870, authors and publishers registered their claims to statutory copyright with the clerks of the U.S. District Court for the jurisdiction in which they resided. Douglass, a former slave who had gained his freedom by fleeing from the south to Pennsylvania, took pains to assert his copyright at a time when slavery was still thriving in parts of the United States. Despite the many hurdles placed in the way of people of colour, copyright could still be harnessed as a means to assert individuality, dignity, and creativity, albeit with difficulty.

Quite apart from issues related to race, copyright also addresses issues of gender equity, although arguably here there is a greater divergence of views. In a blog post I wrote about copyright and feminism,[4] I argued that while there are incontrovertible areas of bias and discrimination against women, such as lower pay for essentially the same work, lower pay in traditionally female-dominated occupations, and fewer opportunities to get into the upper echelons of many businesses and professions, copyright law was not one of them. It is totally gender blind, unlike property or voting laws in the nineteenth and early twentieth centuries or indeed some other laws still in existence today. Promotion of feminism was no doubt the last thing that drafters of the first copyright laws had in mind, but that doesn't mean that the end result was not gender neutral. Women could exercise their copyright at a time when they were denied other property rights, although at times they may have been denied some of the benefits of copyright because of gender-biased contract law.

This blog post generated a fair amount of comment, including one that suggested that the patriarchy did not take the day off when copyright legislation was enacted. If all laws drafted by men are inherently anti-feminist, then one would have to conclude that copyright law falls into this category. Yet it is also a fact that in crafting copyright laws, no reference was made to gender. Copyright laws have always given equal protection to authors, whether they be male or female. In fact, writing is one of the areas

---

4 Hugh Stephens, "Feminism and Copyright Revisited," www.hughstephensblog.net, March 10, 2019; https://hughstephensblog.net/2019/03/10/feminism-and-copyright-revisited/; accessed January 17, 2022.

of early artistic and economic liberation for females (Jane Austen, George Eliot, the Brontë sisters, Louisa May Alcott, et alia). Moreover, unlike other areas of intellectual property, such as patents, where women are underrepresented possibly because of systemic barriers such as registration hurdles, copyright is automatic whether an author is female, male, or non-binary. While there is plenty of evidence of discrimination against females throughout history, I would contend that copyright was not part of it.

Today, small business is an important avenue for minorities and women to advance economically, including individual creators. The digital age has provided small and medium-sized enterprisess, wherever they are located, with the opportunity to reach new markets and audiences, but a framework of fair copyright protection is essential to allow this to happen.

Copyright today is an instrument of empowerment rather than exploitation, part of the solution more than part of the problem. Even though there have been historical injustices, such as with Phillis Wheatley, today copyright can be a liberator and equalizer, putting a powerful tool into the hands of individual creators rather than being part of a system of oppression and exploitation. To cite but one example, an important argument in favour of creating an artists' resale right (see Chapter 7) is that it provides the means for an ongoing transfer of wealth from well-heeled art dealers and collectors in Europe to disadvantaged artists in the developing world. Without copyright, this would not be possible.

SUMMARY

Whether one advances arguments for innovation, jobs, and economic development or moral arguments related to diversity, equity, and cultural sovereignty, copyright is the fuel in the tank that makes all this possible. Piracy is the antithesis of copyright, and its debilitating effects negate the positive elements delivered by copyright: more creative output, reinvestment in new content, and direct and indirect jobs associated with copyright industries. Free riders and value-destroying pirate operations need to be fought on both an industry and government level. Governments need to provide the tools, such as appropriate regulations and legislation, to help legitimate content industries fight back.

Education of consumers can play a role, but in the end, enforcement must be applied to those seeking to profit from the theft of the creative content of others. While different from open piracy, the issue of unauthorized but legal access to content needs to be carefully calibrated. There is clearly a role for access through fair dealing and fair use, but the excessive tilt toward more open access in recent years needs to be re-examined. At the end of the day, removing the incentives to produce new content undermines the very premise for which copyright was established: to "encourage learning" and to "promote the progress of science and useful arts."

CHAPTER 9

Copyright Stories from
the Weekly Blog

FOR THE PAST six-plus years, I have been writing a weekly blog on copyright issues.[1] Some of the blog posts deal with current legal or legislative issues in Canada, the U.S., and elsewhere, but others are inspired by stories that crop up in the press or to which my attention has been drawn by readers. I have excerpted material from some of my blog posts in the chapters of this book to illustrate various points, but in this final chapter I want to share a few of the quirkier blog posts that have been well received by readers, at least to judge by frequency of access. Here is a select sample, slightly edited.

CAILLOU: DID THE LITTLE BOY'S BAD TEMPER SPILL OVER TO THE COPYRIGHT SQUABBLE BETWEEN HIS TWO "MOTHERS"? (APRIL 21. 2021)
Early this year, PBS announced that it would cease carrying the Canadian animated children's TV show *Caillou* (which

1 www.hughstephensblog.net.

means "pebbles" in French) after twenty years on the network. Since *Caillou* is a series not without controversy, some parents no doubt breathed a sigh of relief while others pondered their electronic babysitting options.

To those of you who don't have young children in your life (at the moment or previously), *Caillou* may not be on your radar. There is a whole world out there — characters, vocabulary, controversy — forming part of the children's entertainment scene that is familiar to many and almost unknown to others. If you have had children or looked after young children — those of others, your grandkids, etc. — names like Dora the Explorer, Peppa Pig, Curious George, and, of course, Caillou will be well known to you. How else to get through the period of preparing dinner with a four-year-old around your ankles?

The demise of *Caillou* on PBS — it will continue to be broadcast on the Family Jr. channel in Canada and may be picked up by some other outlet in the U.S. — will no doubt not end the controversy over the main character's behaviour. Parents either love or loathe the little bald boy. *Caillou* was produced between 1997 and 2010 under licence to CINAR and has aired in seventy countries around the world. The books on which the series is based have been translated into over a dozen languages and sold 15 million copies. This makes it one of the most successful Canadian cultural exports, although some who dislike Caillou's behaviour when he is frustrated have wondered whether his occasional histrionics reflect lax parenting standards in Canada. The smouldering discontent with *Caillou* burst into open flames a couple of years ago when he was featured in one of Canada's two national dailies, the *National Post*, under the title, "*Caillou* is an aggressively bad show ruining the world's children ... and it's all Canada's fault."[2]

To parents who don't like *Caillou*'s portrayal of a four-year-old's behaviour, I say, "Change the channel." Maybe four- and five-year-old kids enjoy watching a show that portrays how someone their age actually reacts to things beyond their control rather than having to absorb a morality play. I must say I have never been able to force myself to actually watch a full episode of *Caillou* — although I have read the newspaper or books while it has been on the screen and have thus listened with one ear — but I don't recall anything especially obnoxious. I do recall certain homilies and virtues being emphasized, but I don't think my granddaughter's behaviour was any better or worse for having watched it. All I know is that she enjoyed it and, for a certain period of her young life, when asked what she wanted to watch on TV, the response was invariably, "*Caillou!*"

While *Caillou* has generated lots of controversy among parents and even child psychologists, it also has

---

2 Tristan Hopper, "Caillou is an aggressively bad show ruining the world's children ... and it's all Canada's fault," *National Post*, December 17, 2018; https://nationalpost.com/news/canada/analysis-caillou-is-an-aggressively-bad-show-ruining-the-worlds-children-and-its-all-canadas-fault; accessed January 17, 2022.

an interesting legal and copyright history. *Caillou* was created by Québec writer Christine L'Heureux in 1989. L'Heureux had founded Chouette Publishing two years earlier. The *Caillou* books were illustrated by artist Hélène Desputeaux. Like so many artistic collaborators (Gilbert and Sullivan, Simon and Garfunkel, Abbott and Costello), L'Heureux and Desputeaux had a falling out. And, yes, it was about copyright and money.

As with many cases of this nature, it was complicated. Originally, Chouette Publishing (of which L'Heureux was the majority shareholder) and Desputeaux formed a partnership for the purpose of creating the books. They entered into contracts with each other as co-authors, including assigning the reproduction rights for the use of the Caillou character to Chouette Publishing. This covered merchandising and audiovisual works. Desputeaux was to be paid if she provided illustrations for any works using the character. Moral rights were waived by both parties. Subsequently, there was a dispute over the terms of the contracts. The dispute went to arbitration under Québec's civil code. The arbitrator upheld the contracts, concluded that Chouette held the reproduction rights, and determined that the work was of joint authorship (copyright held jointly) because both parties had signed the contracts as co-authors. Desputeaux's position was that she held the sole copyright for the illustrations of the Caillou character and the character itself.

Desputeaux challenged the arbitral decision and asked the Québec Superior Court to annul it. She argued that the arbitrator had exceeded his mandate and, rather than just ruling on the validity of the contracts, had intervened on the question of intellectual property and the status of the parties as co-authors. Her challenge was dismissed, and the Superior Court upheld the arbitrator's decision. Desputeaux then appealed to the Québec Court of Appeal, where she had better results. The Court of Appeal upheld her appeal, ruling that any determination of copyright fell within the domain of the federal government under the Copyright Act and was not subject to provincial arbitration.

At this point, we need to step back briefly into history and look at the Québec Code of Civil Procedure under which the arbitration took place. The Québec civil code goes back to the Québec Act of 1774, which reinstated French law in civil matters as part of an attempt to win the loyalty of French Canadians by preserving the French language and French institutions (civil law and the role of the church) after the British won the Battle of the Plains of Abraham in September 1759. British law had prevailed during the brief period between 1763, when France ceded control of Québec to Britain, and the passage of the Québec Act. A civil code ultimately based on the Napoleonic Codes in France was formally adopted in Québec (Lower Canada) in the 1860s and, with minor changes and updates, has prevailed there ever since, operating alongside British criminal and federal law. The civil code required arbitration in matters of disputes between professional artists and promoters.

With the provincial Court of Appeal having ruled in favour of Desputeaux, L'Heureux and the publishing company appealed that decision to the Supreme Court of Canada. The Supreme Court ultimately determined that the federal Copyright Act does not prevent an arbitrator from ruling on the question of copyright.[3] The arbitrator's mandate includes everything closely connected with the agreement under adjudication, and, in this particular case, the issue of co-authorship was intrinsically related to other questions raised within the terms of the agreement. Even though copyright affirms rights against all third parties globally, two parties to a copyright dispute should not be denied the right to arbitration, the court ruled. L'Heureux's appeal and joint authorship was upheld.

It doesn't end there, however. Two years after the ruling, the two parties were back in court again. They finally reached an agreement, which remained confidential for ten years until it was released in 2015. This agreement affirmed Desputeaux's rights to her original illustrations of Caillou but gave Chouette permission to license and create subsequent versions, including through its agreement with CINAR for the animated television production. Desputeaux was to be granted a percentage of the royalties. Desputeaux agreed to limit production of Caillou depictions for a five-year period. Was this the end to the dispute? Regrettably, it was not.

3 Desputeaux v Éditions Chouette (1987) inc., 2003 scc 17, March 21, 2003; https://scc-csc.lexum.com/scc-csc/scc-csc/en/item/2048/index.do; accessed January 17, 2022.

Desputeaux subsequently applied for a judicial declaration that L'Heureux had no claim to co-authorship of Caillou following the 2005 settlement agreement. She wanted the court to declare that the 2005 settlement agreement prevailed over the original arbitral decision and that its terms precluded L'Heureux from claiming moral rights in the works or being co-author. The application was dismissed in November 2018 on the basis that it was a disguised form of appeal of a case that had already been decided by the Supreme Court.

How is it all going to end? I know that Caillou believes in sharing because I have heard him say so. But what constitutes a fair share can depend on your perspective, which perhaps explains why Caillou's bad temper seems to have rubbed off on his creators. More than two decades of copyright litigation has surrounded this little character who continues to enthrall or enrage parents and kids — and his co-authors as well. Maybe there is a moral lesson hidden in there after all.

A COPYRIGHT CONTROVERSY: THE GIANT RUBBER DUCKY IS BACK (MAY 23, 2016)

Since this blog was written in 2016, the Giant Rubber Ducky seems to have lost its allure. It was popping up everywhere for a while. Wherever it went, it caused copyright waves.

There was no ducking it. In March 2016, Dutch artist Florentijn Hofman's giant rubber ducky creation was back in the news, once again at the centre of a controversy over copyright. This time, the duck had surfaced in Brazil, where a group protesting government corruption and high taxes was using a version of Hofman's giant duck (but with crosses for eyes) to send a message to the government. Written across its chest was the slogan "*Chega de pagar o pato,*" a Portuguese expression literally meaning, "We won't pay for the duck anymore." To non-Brazilians, this may seem like a strange expression, but I am informed by a Portuguese-speaking friend that "paying the duck" means that the duck has to be compensated for being eaten, and the slogan is meant to convey the point that the duck (which represents the people of Brazil) is being consumed by corruption. The colloquial translation is "we will no longer pay for what is not our fault" or "we won't take the blame any longer."

Hofman claimed the duck was an exact replica of his design and constituted copyright infringement. The Brazilian protesters could perhaps have responded that they were making legitimate use of copyright exceptions by indulging in satire or parody. A parody exception apparently exists in Brazilian copyright law and would be an interesting defence if indeed there were a violation of copyright law. Although one can debate whether Hofman's design is original (in that he has made a very large version of a common design), this was not the first time that his giant duck had been involved in a copyright dispute.

In June 2015, at the Philadelphia Tall Ships Festival, Hofman's giant duck appeared without his authorization.

He had licensed his designs to a firm organizing the Los Angeles Tall Ships Festival the previous year, and this firm, which was also the producer of the Philly event, produced another giant duck for Philadelphia. The producer claimed that even though the Los Angeles organizers had paid Hofman for his design and credited it to him on the LA Tall Ships website, the one in Philadelphia was "not his [Hofman's] duck" but "just another large inflatable duck." Perhaps it was poetic justice that the Philly duck didn't stand up to expectations and suffered an irremediable tear, a deflating experience for the children of Philadelphia who had come to see it.

In 2013, the duck had sailed into controversy in Asia. Problems cropped up in Taiwan, where Hofman complained of unauthorized rubber duck–themed merchandise being circulated, including duck-design stored-value cards used for transportation or other payments issued by the Taiwan Smart Card Corp. It also made headlines in mainland China. After an authorized version of Hofman's giant duck appeared in Hong Kong harbour, knockoffs quickly appeared in several Chinese cities, prompting the *China Daily* to highlight fears of copyright violation.[4] The duck became a symbol of the differences between Hong Kong (an autonomous part of China under the "one country, two systems" principle developed when Britain returned

4 Zhao Yinan and Wang Yuke, "Ducks Trigger Copyright Fears," *China Daily USA*, June 4, 2013; http://usa.chinadaily.com.cn/china/2013-06/04 /content_16562722.htm; accessed January 17, 2022.

the territory to Chinese rule in 1997), where intellectual property rights are generally respected, and China proper, where intellectual property rights are often perceived as more of a nuisance than something to be respected and paid for. Even within China, the more sophisticated cities looked down their noses at their country cousins who sought to duplicate Hong Kong's success on the cheap, and Beijing proudly announced that the real rubber duck, with Hofman as escort, would be coming to China's capital city as part of Beijing Design Week.

With all the controversy, the burning question was whether Hofman was really the owner of a copyrighted work with his giant duck design, and whether those making similar large inflatable rubber ducks were violating his copyright. The issue was considered by such respected publications as the *Journal of Intellectual Property Law and Property*[5] (inconclusive) and the Latin American legal website IP Tango,[6] which concluded that in Brazil Hofman's duck would not be protected as an industrial design, but the technical drawings might constitute an artistic work worthy of protection. Beijing Design Week's organizing

---

5 Earl Grey and Raymond Scott, "Blowing the whistle on copyright in public sculptures," *Journal of Intellectual Property Law & Practice* (2014) doi: 10.1093/jiplp/jpu194, first published online: October 14, 2014: http:// jiplp.blogspot.com/2014/10/blowing-whistle-on-copyright-in-public.html; accessed January 17, 2022.

6 Patricia Covarubbia, "Check your rubber duck: is it original?" IP Tango, April 12, 2016; https://iptango.blogspot.com/2016/04/check-your -rubber-duck-is-it-original.html; accessed January 17, 2022.

committee made copyright protection of Hofman's work a focus of its event, and in Taiwan the director general of the Taiwan Intellectual Property Office is reported to have said that it is highly likely that due to its creativity, Hofman's rubber duck would have copyright protection there. Back in Philadelphia, however, intellectual property attorney Jordan LaVine was quoted as being very skeptical that the work had sufficient originality for copyright to be attached to it.[7] He pointed out, "A rubber duck is an extremely common thing and making a very large one does not necessarily give someone copyright rights in that artistic expression." In fact, according to the National Toy Hall of Fame,[8] small rubber ducks have been around since the late nineteenth century (they originally did not float) and have been floating in bathtubs since at least the 1940s.

All this uncertainty was bound to attract the attention of some aspiring copyright lawyer. It is the sort of case that could float or deflate a career. While we can all have a bit of fun with Hofman's duck (he has created other massive inflatable sculptures as well, which are more original in design), the controversy does raise some serious issues

7   Victor Fiorillo, "Dutch Rubber Duck Artist Cries Foul Over Giant Philly Rubber Duck," *Philadelphia Magazine*, June 2, 2015; https://www .phillymag.com/news/2015/06/02/philadelphia-rubber-duck-dutch-artist/; accessed January 17, 2022.

8   Rubber Duck, Strong National Museum of Play, https://www.museum ofplay.org/toys/rubber-duck/; accessed March 26, 2023; PBS, " Rubber duck, chess inducted into Toy Hall of Fame," November 7, 2013; https:// www.pbs.org/newshour/nation/rubber-duck-chess-inducted-into-toy-hall -of-fame; accessed March 26, 2023

about the rights of creators and when and how they are to be compensated for their original works. If nothing else, Hofman brought that issue into the spotlight for all of us to consider.

COPYRIGHT AND YOUR CARBON FOOTPRINT
(APRIL 1, 2019, AND MAY 18, 2020)

Copyright has many dimensions, but who would have thought that there was an ecological component to it? Well, there is. Here I combine edited content from two blog posts, one written in 2019 and the other during the COVID pandemic in May 2020, when many people were shut inside and listening to music, especially on vinyl, had become a thing.

I live in a very "green" part of the world, British Columbia. Despite being a resource-based economy for the better part of a century and a half, BC is beginning to transition to a clean, knowledge-based economy. And what could be better positioned to be at the cutting edge of a knowledge-based, green, environmentally friendly transition than the copyright industries? Vancouver is not known as Hollywood North for nothing, with film production reported to have contributed $3.4 billion (USD $2.58 billion) to the provincial economy in 2017–18. But are copyright industries really all that green? While copyright products consist of intangible intellectual property, their production still requires consumption of physical resources and thus has a carbon footprint.

This dilemma was brought home to me forcefully by a fascinating analysis of the carbon footprint of music, written by two researchers at Keele University in the UK.[9] The authors, Sharon George and Deirdre McKay, compared the carbon footprint and "greenness" of various music formats, including online streaming. They point out that the surge in popularity of vinyl records, made with PVC instead of the more environmentally friendly shellac of earlier generations, has led to an increased environmental impact: "Modern records typically contain around 135g of PVC material with a carbon footprint of 0.5kg of carbon dioxide (based on 3.4kg of CO_2 per 1kg of PVC). Sales of 4.1m records would produce 1.9 thousand tonnes of CO_2 — not taking transport and packaging into account. That is the entire carbon footprint of almost four hundred people per year."

Vinyl is not a clean technology, and vinyl is now making a comeback, outselling CDs on a revenue basis.[10] It's not just that vinyl is an oil-based product, thus adding to our consumption of fossil fuels, but the pellets that feed the pressing process come mainly from one supplier, the Thai Petrochemical Corporation in Bangkok, a company

9   Sharon George and Deirdre McKay, "The Environmental Impact of Music: Digital, Records, CDs Analysed," The Conversation, January 18, 2019; https://www.keele.ac.uk/about/news/2019/january/music /environmental-impact.php; accessed January 17, 2022.

10   Scott Nover, "Vinyl outsold CDs in the U.S. for the first time in decades," Quartz, January 11, 2022; https://qz.com/2111339/vinyl-outsold -cds-in-the-us-for-the-first-time-since-the-1980s/; accessed January 17, 2022.

with a less than stellar environmental record that has been accused by Greenpeace of dumping toxic effluent into the Chao Praya River.[11]

What is the solution? Some purists have suggested that consumers return to the shellac records (the old 78 LPS) that prevailed until the mid-twentieth century, since shellac is a renewable resource and is biodegradable. Shellac comes from the lac beetle, which deposits a sticky residue on the branches of trees in South Asia, where the residue is harvested by hand. After collection, it is melted and crushed. During the period when shellac was widely produced, exploitation of Third World labour was notorious in the industry. But shellac wasn't the only ingredient in the discs. It was the binding agent for a variety of fillers ranging from limestone to asbestos, asphalt, caustic soda, cement, flour, and formaldehyde. A real witches' brew. So perhaps going back to shellac records is not the answer. Like vinyl, cassettes and CDs are also plastic based; in fact, the packaging of a CD is a bigger user of hydrocarbons than the disc inside, and as cassettes and now CDs lose their popularity, a lot of plastic ends up in landfills.

According to George and McKay: "CDs are made of layered polycarbonate and aluminium, which has slightly less environmental impact than PVC, and are manufactured using less materials than records. However, CDs can't be recycled because they're made of mixed materials, which

11   Kyle Devine, "Decomposed: The Political Ecology of Music," Cambridge, MA, MIT Press, 2019, pp. 2–7.

are difficult and uneconomical to separate into their component parts for recycling."

CDs have largely been replaced by downloading and
streaming, where there is no physical medium. Surely, this
must be much more environmentally friendly. The only
trouble is, as our researchers point out, "Even though new
formats are material-free, that doesn't mean they don't
have an environmental impact. The electronic files we
download are stored on active, cooled servers."

Those servers burn a lot of energy. One report indicates that the amount of energy consumed by the world's
data centres will treble in the next decade. This will put an
enormous strain on energy supplies and increase consumption of fossil fuels in order to create electricity, producing
more carbon. There is even a suggestion that the amount
of electricity consumed to keep the internet operating may
have finite limits. Streaming is now increasingly replacing
downloading as a way of consuming music, but the Keele
University researchers noted that streaming music may not
be the most environmentally friendly, carbon-reducing
option for distribution. If you like only a few tracks and
play them repeatedly, it is more environmentally effective
to play them on your CD player, which consumes less electricity than the infrastructure necessary to support your
streaming of the track each time you want to hear it. In
fact, the electricity consumption is about one-third less
annually to play a CD for the same number of hours as
streaming the content. According to George and McKay,

even if you include the carbon cost of producing the physical CD, there comes a break-even point when the carbon footprint of manufacturing the CD and its player, and then playing the disc, is less than streaming the content. According to them, "Streaming an album over the internet more than twenty-seven times will likely use more energy than it takes to produce and manufacture a CD."

That's how to deal with music and stay green, but what about audiovisual content? Audiovisual files are much higher consumers of bandwidth, especially if they are in high-definition format, so should we eschew streaming for downloading videos or purchasing discs? Maybe streaming is a more environmentally friendly option because people consume visual content much differently than music. Once you have binged *Game of Thrones*, you aren't likely to watch it over and over again, as is the case with favoured music tracks. It's usually a one-time thing. Of course, there are exceptions, like children's movies, which your kids may want to watch again and again and again.

There is no question that digital technology has changed the movie industry and reduced its carbon footprint. Now digital files can be flashed around the world instead of using the cumbersome process of printing and shipping 35-millimetre celluloid film prints. The shift to digital has been a recent phenomenon; it not only saves the studios millions of dollars a year in producing prints but eliminates the manufacturing process and consumption of materials. Offsetting those savings, of course, are the costs of all those energy-sucking server farms. Digital photos have had the same impact in terms of reducing the need for film and the developing and printing of most photographs, reducing requirements for plastics, chemicals, and specialized paper, as Kodak found to its chagrin.

If music, movies, and photography, three very important copyright industries, have their own carbon footprint, what about book and magazine publishing? If server farms and data centres indirectly emit a lot of carbon dioxide because of their energy consumption, does that make e-books less green than the traditional hard copies? Books and magazines come with the additional environmental impact of cutting down trees and processing them into paper, although an increasing number are now made with recycled materials. Hardcover books are hard to recycle because of the backing and the glue, but then many books have a long shelf life. You can lend them, donate them to a library, give them away in a book drive, or build a personal library. Intuitively, I would think that e-books have a smaller footprint, but there is something about the heft of a solid book.

Given the above, can I hold up my end while still patronizing and supporting copyright industries? I hope so and will continue to do my best to be copyright-green. Given that my bookshelves are already full, I will try to borrow more from the library, and I will of course walk or cycle to get there. I will stream where I can and download or purchase discs only where that seems to be a less carbon-intensive option. I will try to be energy-efficient, and I may even plant a tree as an offset to all that production of carbon for which as a consumer I am responsible. What I won't do is stop consuming music, films, and books. After all, they are what make life worth living.

HAPPY BIRTHDAY (FEBRUARY 14, 2016)
This was the first blog post that I published, back in February 2016. It is a story of something losing its copyright coverage, but since we all sing "Happy Birthday," it is a story worth recounting. For many years, the song was assumed to be protected by a copyright, although it was never a factor when the song was sung at private parties. Licensing was only relevant for commercial uses, such as featuring the song in a film. It turns out, however, that the copyright registration was faulty and was challenged in court. It is one of the interesting twists and turns of copyright.

News of Warner/Chappell's $14-million settlement of the "Happy Birthday" copyright suit made headlines worldwide.[12] It is a story that everyone can relate to. The decision by Warner Music Group, parent of music publisher Warner/Chappell, to make this substantial payment (assuming the judge in the case agrees) to settle a lawsuit brought against it for enforcing its copyright over the lyrics to the popular song was based on the decision of a California court in 2015, which ruled that Warner's claim to the copyright was

---

12 Jana Kasperkevic, "Music publisher agrees to pay $14m to end Happy Birthday song lawsuit," *The Guardian*, February 9, 2016; https://www
.theguardian.com/business/2016/feb/09/happy-birthday-song-lawsuit
-warner-chappell-settlement; accessed January 17, 2022.

invalid. It is a complicated story, in which researchers had to find proof that the song was publicly published prior to the registration of copyright on the lyrics in 1935. A crucial piece of evidence was a 1922 songbook containing the lyrics to "Happy Birthday," absent of any reference to copyright.

Warner had acquired the rights to the song when it purchased Birchtree Ltd. for some $25 million in 1988. Birchtree was an educational music company that had acquired the original catalogue from the company that registered the copyright for "Happy Birthday" in 1935, the Clayton F. Summy Company. The lawsuit challenging its copyright was brought against Warner/Chappell in 2013 by filmmaker Jennifer Nelson, who objected to paying the $1,500 royalty that the putative rights holder required for licensing the lyrics for use in the documentary film she was making on the origins of the popular song.

Naturally, the plaintiffs were delighted at their victory. Beyond the plaintiffs, however, many commentators have claimed that the case illustrated major problems with copyright law and demonstrated that copyright terms are too long. According to the anti-copyright Electronic Frontier Foundation, "it's too easy for concentrated copyright interests, even invalid ones, to beat back the diffuse public interest."[13] But is this in fact the case? I would strongly contend the opposite.

13 Parker Higgins, "Happy Birthday To Everybody: Victory For The Public Domain (With An Asterisk)," EFF, September 23, 2015; https://www.eff.org/deeplinks/2015/09/happy-birthday-everybody-victory-public-domain-asterisk; accessed January 17, 2022.

The story is long and convoluted. The original piano arrangement of a melody with different lyrics set to the music was created by Mildred Jane Hill and Patty Smith Hill, two teachers of early childhood education in the U.S. in the 1890s. Many years later, in 1934, after the words of "Happy Birthday" were set to this tune and it became popular in movies and even a Broadway show without any credit to the Hill sisters, a younger sister, Jessica, filed for copyright in conjunction with Clayton Summy, a music publisher. The copyright was granted. A share of the proceeds from the royalties has been administered ever since through the Hill Foundation for the benefit of the heirs of Mildred and Patty Hill, as copyright law is intended to do. The fact that Warner/Chappell in good faith purchased the rights to the song for a not inconsiderable sum, which was based in part on the anticipated revenue flow from the portfolio they purchased, does not in the least invalidate the application of copyright in this instance. At the time of purchase (and subsequently), Warner/Chappell had every right to expect that the copyright was legitimate since it had been in existence unchallenged for over fifty years, with royalties being collected regularly.

It is reported that Warner/Chappell was generating about $2 million dollars per year in licensing fees from the copyright. Given that the $25 million they paid in 1988 is worth approximately double that amount in current dollars, and given estimates that up to a third of the value of Birchtree resided in the "Happy Birthday" copyright, then $2 million per year in royalties does not seem out of line. In fact, it would have taken Warner/Chappell roughly eight years to earn back the cost of purchasing the copyright before they turned a nickel of profit. Reportedly, Nelson was asked to pay $1,500 for the use of the song in her film, and it was this request that ultimately led to the lawsuit. In the past, others have refrained from using the song in their productions in order to avoid payment to Warner/Chappell, which leads to the question of what is the optimal charge for licensing a popular song? Is it better to grant ten licenses at $500 or two licenses at $1,500? What will the market bear? That is a commercial decision for the rights holder to make, and it is entirely within their purview to do so, popular song or not. They could have charged less; they could have charged more.

So, while some commentators claim this case is further proof that copyright law is out of step with today's world and that there was something almost immoral in charging license fees for a popular copyrighted work, in fact it proves just the opposite. It demonstrates that the legal process related to upholding or challenging copyrights operates as intended. In this case, while Warner/Chappell not unreasonably sought to earn a return on its investment, it was ultimately shown to have a legally tenuous claim to the copyright over the lyrics of the song (despite common acceptance of the validity of the copyright over many years) on the basis of new evidence. If the decision had gone the other way, as well it could have, the critics no doubt would have been crying foul. Given the result, they are crowing, but the fact that the plaintiffs were upheld is based exclusively on the merits of this particular case and has nothing to do with the underlying validity or concept of copyright.

The main conclusion I draw from the "Happy Birthday" judgment is that it is important to register copyright properly and ensure that the registration is properly documented. The passage of time and customary acceptance is clearly not sufficient to withstand a legal challenge.

AY, THERE'S THE RUB: WHEN YOU CANNOT (OR SHOULD NOT) COPY SOMETHING DESPITE ITS LACK OF COPYRIGHT PROTECTION (JANUARY 18, 2021)

For this selection, I have chosen a post that discusses one of the key issues raised in Chapter 7 regarding the limits of copyright. In this case, it concerns the question of how to protect Indigenous works, even though legally they may not be protected by copyright.

Several decades ago, in my younger days, my wife and I spent a summer in England visiting the many historical sites of that great country. During the trip, we visited a number of cathedrals. I don't remember them all, but Winchester was one for sure. I still have vivid memories of young students sprawled out on the floor of the cathedral taking rubbings from the brass effigies of knights and clergy inlaid in the stone floor. That was a popular pastime in the 1960s and 1970s — and earlier, going back to the Victorian era. Today, it is discouraged because of the impact on the integrity of the originals from repeated rubbings. It can still be done, but normally from reproductions, such as those found at St. Martin-in-the-Fields in London, where reproductions of famous effigies from throughout England have been collected so tourists can take rubbings from them. You can also buy reproductions of the rubbings for a modest sum.

My mind flashed back to those tomb rubbings when I recently visited Gabriola Island, one of the southern Gulf Islands in the Salish Sea between Vancouver Island and the mainland of British Columbia. Gabriola is home to more than seventy petroglyphs, rock carvings executed by the Indigenous people of the area, the Snuneymuxw (pronounced Snoo-nai-mu), over many hundreds of years. While it is hard to date the carvings, most are believed to be several hundred years old or older, although some may be of relatively recent vintage. They depict wildlife and anthropomorphic figures and are scattered around the island, some near the coast, others in auspicious rocky areas, most on what is now considered private land.

Given the attraction of the petroglyphs, and in order to prevent damage to the originals, a few years ago, a project was started to make casts of most of the glyphs to display on the grounds of the local museum, laid out on the ground amongst the trees. As they soon became covered in the soft moss typical of the island, they took on the aura of the originals. People, especially student groups, were encouraged to visit the castings and the museum to learn the history of the Snuneymuxw people, and as part of the educational experience, they were allowed — even encouraged — to take rubbings of the images displayed in the reproduced castings. The museum even supplied rubbing kits for a small fee.

That was back in the 1990s. Now the signs encouraging the making of rubbings have been painted over, and the rubbing kits are no longer for sale. The Gabriola Museum has posted a sign saying that after consultation with the Snuneymuxw Nation, the taking of rubbings from the castings is no longer permitted. Why the change? After all, these are "just" reproductions. And aren't they public domain works? They are not protected by any form of copyright.

To answer this question, we need to look deeper at the origin and meaning of the glyphs and to understand the broader global context regarding the protection of Indigenous cultural expression. Many countries are grappling with how to adapt copyright laws to protect this form of expression. One solution may be an international treaty that has been under negotiation at the World Intellectual Property Organization for a number of years, the Treaty on Intellectual Property and Genetic Resources, Traditional Knowledge and Folklore,[14] but this is a slow process that ultimately may not be productive. Another solution might

---

14 World Intellectual Property Organization, "The WIPO Intergovernmental Committee on Intellectual Property and Genetic Resources, Traditional Knowledge and Folklore," https://www.wipo.int/edocs/pubdocs/en/wipo _pub_tk_2.pdf; accessed November 3, 2022.

be to establish a rights management agency for Indigenous culture, along the lines of what is being considered in Canada. This would allow users to gain consent and license the use of protected cultural expressions (images, designs, music, dances, and so on) while at the same time protecting them and restricting their use, even if they are not subject to copyright.

A key piece of the puzzle is the UN Declaration on the Rights of Indigenous Peoples,[15] which has been endorsed by 144 countries, including the U.S. and Canada. The declaration — although not binding in domestic law in many countries, including, unfortunately, the U.S. and Canada — gives Indigenous peoples the right to maintain, control, protect, and develop cultural heritage including literature, designs, visual and performing arts, and other aspects of traditional knowledge.

In line with the right to control and protect cultural artifacts, it may be that some are considered so sacred that they should not be reproduced at all. There are numerous petroglyph sites in the U.S. (in Arizona, New Mexico, Nevada, Utah, Washington, Illinois, Michigan, Missouri, and Hawaii), and there is a major petroglyph site in eastern Canada, north of Toronto. At Petroglyphs Provincial Park, all the glyphs are protected by a weatherproof building, and even photography of the images is not allowed. At

15 United Nations Department of Economic and Social Affairs-Indigenous Peoples, "United Nations Declaration on the Rights of Indigenous Peoples," https://www.un.org/development/desa/indigenouspeoples/declaration -on-the-rights-of-indigenous-peoples.html; accessed November 3, 2022.

the Petroglyphs National Monument in New Mexico, the National Parks Service has this advice for visitors: "We encourage you to respect the beliefs of the descendants of those who carved the images on the rocks. The petroglyphs within the park are sacred to many people living in the area today. Out of respect and consideration of present-day peoples, we currently do not post any images on our website or place any images in our publications that display the human form. We would encourage you not to use the images for commercial purposes."

As you can see, if even photography is often not allowed or is constrained, it is understandable that taking rubbings, even of reproductions, can cross the line of what is acceptable. There is obviously a balance somewhere between limiting access and reproduction for spiritual reasons and promoting dissemination of the images for purposes of education and awareness.

It seems to me that the Snuneymuxw people and the Gabriola Museum have been able to find that balance by keeping reproductions of the glyphs on display in a natural and respectful setting — along with providing suitable explanations and interpretative materials — while avoiding demeaning the symbolism of the images by allowing them to become a form of children's activity or entertainment.

As for the connection with copyright: while copyright law cannot be invoked to prevent unauthorized reproduction in this case — it's just not the right instrument — many of the principles of copyright, including the concept of moral rights, are in play here. (The Snuneymuxw have, however, registered ten of the images as trademarked designs.) Fundamentally, it is a question of respect: respect for the artist (or artists) who created the work and respect for the meaning and essence of the work. While the artists who created the glyphs are not in a position to give or withhold permission to use or reproduce them, the stewards of the works (the current leaders of the community or First Nation) are entitled to do so. To me, that is similar to basic elements of copyright — respect for the results of creative endeavour through appropriate use with permission.

COPYRIGHTING THE OGOPOGO MONSTER: THE © STORY BEHIND THE NEWS STORY (NOVEMBER 1, 2022)

This blog post appeared as a guest article on the British IP website IP Kat.

The headline — "City of Vernon transfers copyright to legendary Ogopogo to BC Indigenous nations" — was featured in newspapers and broadcasts across Canada, based on a Canadian Press article.[16] For the uninitiated, Ogopogo is Canada's version of the Loch Ness Monster, supposedly residing in the depths of Lake Okanagan in the interior of British Columbia, near the City of Vernon.

The City of Vernon's decision was certainly consistent with the current spirit of reconciliation with Canada's First

---

16 Dirk Meissner, Canadian Press. October 16, 2021; https://globalnews.ca /news/8271245/ogopogo-copyright-transferred-okanagan-nation-alliance; accessed April 30, 2023.

Nations, but something didn't seem right. How could the City of Vernon own the rights to a mythical lake creature similar to the Loch Ness Monster? Surely no author had created the Ogopogo (supposedly a green, serpent-like creature that creates harmonic ripples as it swims), so no one could claim copyright.

Perhaps the right involved was actually a trademark registration, and the journalist had got it wrong? A press report indicated the registration had been made in 1953 by Arthur "Gil" Seabrook, a local broadcaster, as a civic promotion. He subsequently assigned his rights to the City of Vernon. Seabrook's 2010 obituary says, "... as a marketing / promotion effort, he personally obtained the registered trademark for the word 'Ogopogo' and an artistic rendering of the famed lake monster. This, much to the chagrin of [...] other Okanagan cities. Eventually the rights to use 'Ogopogo' were offered to the City of Vernon, where it remained dormant ..."[17]

The author decided to search the Canadian Trademark Database for information on what had been registered under the mark "Ogopogo." He found seventeen entries related to a range of products including books, wine, chocolates, suntan products, clothing, and soft drinks. There are also many businesses that use the name without registration, such as Ogopogo Giftland, Ogopogo Lawn Sprinklers, and the Ogopogo Motel. Many of the marks

17 *Vernon Morning Star*, November 28, 2010; https://www.vernonmorning star.com/obituaries/arthur-gilbert-gill-seabrook/; accessed November 3, 2022.

had lapsed due to non-renewal, and none was in the name of the City of Vernon.

He then searched the Copyright Database maintained by the Canadian Intellectual Property Office (CIPO). There were eighteen registered copyrighted works related to the word Ogopogo, including books, posters, artwork, videos (in some cases, supposedly of the creature itself), and dramatic works. But since it is not compulsory to register a copyright, there are likely more unregistered works out there based on Ogopogo that are subject to copyright protection. The database only goes back to 1991.

So, what did Seabrook register under copyright? Unfortunately, while CIPO's database records registration, it has no copy of what was registered.

The Ogopogo trademark (or copyright) had apparently remained dormant after Seabrook transferred it to the City of Vernon. Thirty years later, in 1984, local author Don Levers wrote a self-published children's book called *Ogopogo: The Misunderstood Lake Monster* that sold well. Levers had heard the stories about Vernon owning the Ogopogo copyright, so, playing safe, he asked for permission to use it in his book, which was freely granted.

Fast forward to March 2021, and Levers decided to publish a sequel, this time with a publisher. Once again, city council was approached for permission to use Ogopogo. Press reports incorrectly stated permission was required "because the city has the copyright to the word

Ogopogo." Once again, the council agreed, but that was when the issue of cultural appropriation came to the fore.

The City of Vernon's heretofore long-forgotten and dormant copyright ownership was suddenly — and uncomfortably —put into the spotlight. Questions were raised about why the City of Vernon held title to the name "Ogopogo" when it was based on a native legend. Didn't the Syilx First Nation really own Ogopogo?

The Guardian picked up the story,[18] framing it as an Indigenous nation trying to reclaim its culture. Vernon's city council quickly decided to relinquish its copyright and assign it to the Okanagan Nation Alliance. The *Globe and Mail* reported, "For $1, council voted to assign and transfer to the Okanagan Nation Alliance all copyright, title, interest and property including trademark rights arising from the commercial and non-commercial use of the Ogopogo name."[19]

Except that is not exactly what happened, as the City of Vernon council minutes make clear. What was transferred was all copyright, title, etc. "in the Work," not the name Ogopogo. So, what was the work registered under Copyright #102327 on June 9, 1953? We may never know.

The original copyright certificate simply says that

18 Leyland Cecco, "'Like copyrighting Moses': hands off our water spirit, say First Nations," *The Guardian*, April 6, 2021; https://www.theguardian.com/world/2021/apr/06/ogopogo-sacred-water-spirit-indigenous-canada; accessed November 3, 2022.

19 Meissner, *Globe and Mail*, October 16, 2021.

Seabrook registered an "unpublished literary and artistic work entitled Ogopogo." An unpublished work can be copyrighted as long as it is fixed, but since it was unpublished, it may no longer exist. And remember, when a work is registered with CIPO, no copies are retained. The City of Vernon appears to have no idea of what the work contains, and Seabrook is no longer around to ask.

Why did Levers's publisher approach the City of Vernon to clear the copyright in 2021, when over the years multiple books have been published about Ogopogo without doing so? After all, the City of Vernon only owned the copyright to an unpublished work. Apparently, it was out of an excess of caution and due diligence, just in case there might be a challenge.

Once Levers's publisher finally got a look at the rights held by the City of Vernon, they realized no permission was required. Nothing in Seabrook's unpublished work was used in the sequel. The copyright approval request would have been a non-issue if the media had not jumped on the reconciliation angle.

Although the City of Vernon never had the copyright to the name Ogopogo, its renunciation makes a good hook for a story about reconciliation. The Okanagan Nation appreciated the gesture, even if all they actually got for $1 were the rights to an unpublished work. More important, perhaps, they got recognition of the fact that the lake creature is indelibly linked to their traditional culture and an acceptance that they should have some say over it.

There is one final, ironic point regarding the name Ogopogo. Although Native groups had an oral tradition of a lake creature, it had an entirely different name. It was known as N'ha-a-itk and was probably never considered by the original peoples as an actual creature but rather the spirit of the lake.

According to the BBC,[20] the name Ogopogo was actually conferred by tourism officials in the 1920s and drawn from an old English music hall song.

The N'ha-a-itk of the Syilix and the Ogopogo that was labelled by officials keen to promote tourism have become very different things, although springing originally from the same source. You cannot put that genie back in the bottle. For better or for worse, the well-known Ogopogo name and image will continue to adorn wine bottles, boxes of chocolates, motels and RV parks, bed-and-breakfast establishments, a stucco and masonry business, a gymnasium, a moving and storage outfit — even an air cadet squadron — and will continue to feature in books, plays, and artwork.

If the City of Vernon did not hold the copyright to the name Ogopogo, then neither does the Okanagan Nation Alliance, despite the assignment of whatever rights the City of Vernon had (or thought it had). People remain free to continue to express their own ideas and tell stories of

20 Lisa Kadane, "Canada's mysterious lake monster," BBC March 10, 2020; https://www.bbc.com/travel/article/20200309-ogopogo-the-monster -lurking-in-okanagan-lake; accessed November 3, 2022.

what the Lake Okanagan water spirit is and what its characteristics are. They can also continue to copyright those artistic expressions and creations, but hopefully will do so in a way that is respectful of the creature's cultural context and history.

THE MICKEY MOUSE COPYRIGHT EXTENSION MYTH: A CONVENIENT STRAW MAN TO ATTACK, (MAY 16, 2022)

The Walt Disney Company has often been accused by opponents of copyright of being an attack dog when it comes to copyright litigation. There is no question that the company, like others, takes pains to assert and protect its rights, which is only natural, considering that content is the essence of the Disney corporation. It is very protective of its intellectual property. But one particularly unfair label that has been pinned on Disney, specifically on that Disney icon Mickey Mouse, is calling the U.S. Copyright Term Extension Act of 1998, which brought the U.S. term of protection into alignment with that of the EU, the "Mickey Mouse Term Extension Act." So visceral is the opposition to Disney in some quarters that Republicans in the House and Senate who consider the company too politically correct or "woke" introduced legislation to deny any further extensions of Disney's copyright on the Mouse. The copyright on Mickey's first animated cartoon, "Steamboat Willie", expires on January 1, 2024. The legislation was a meaningless piece of political theatre, as I explained in the following blog post.

The Walt Disney Company has delighted generations of children and adults with its style of wholesome family entertainment, whether movies, cartoons, games, or theme parks. That's the Disney brand. Disney has generally managed to steer clear of political controversies and stay safely in the middle ground, very much in the mainstream. Like any global corporation, Disney needs to satisfy a range of stakeholders, the most important of whom are its customers, but also including, of course, shareholders, employees, and regulatory authorities. Disney has managed to navigate these sometimes conflicting demands pretty well. After all, it has successfully established theme parks in places as varied (in terms of political environment and regulatory expectations) as Paris, Tokyo, Hong Kong, and Shanghai. Not to mention Anaheim, California, and Orlando, Florida. Florida might be the most challenging regulatory environment in which it operates.

In 2022, Disney was targeted by some state and federal Republican officials because they felt Disney was not on board with Florida's Parental Rights in Education Bill (a.k.a. the "Don't Say Gay" bill). If adopted, it would prevent discussion of sexual orientation or gender identity instruction in Florida classrooms from kindergarten through grade three. Disney would no doubt prefer to avoid wading into a controversial issue like this that is unrelated to its business, but the unhappiness of some Disney employees over its initial low profile led the company to take a corporate position against the bill.

It is not my intention to step into the minefield of Florida, or gender identity, politics. Disney is more than capable of defending itself and explaining its corporate positions. Rather, I want to highlight the ludicrous position taken by some political critics of Disney to try to punish the company by attacking it on the basis of its copyright holdings. Two Republican members of the U.S. House of Representatives, Rep. Jim Banks of Indiana and Rep. Jim Jordan of Ohio, threatened to block any extension of Disney's copyright on Mickey Mouse.

That might have been a real threat if Disney had actually been seeking to extend the term of protection of U.S. copyright law, which of course would apply to everyone, not just Disney. But there was no suggestion that they were. Nor was anyone else attempting to achieve this. Banks wrote to Disney's CEO, opposing any extension to Disney's copyrights — extensions that Disney had not asked for. This must be the straw man of all straw men.

The next development was that Senator Josh Hawley (R-MO), in a publicity stunt designed to punish Disney, introduced the Copyright Clause Restoration Act (S-4178), which would specifically target the Walt Disney Company by rolling back existing copyright protection on its works along with drastically shortening the term of copyright protection for all other copyright holders going forward. Apart from being an unconstitutional expropriation of property, the bill would put the U.S. in violation of commitments made in a number of bilateral and multilateral trade agreements, notably the conditions of its accession to the Berne Convention.

The retroactive and expropriative element of the bill was worded so that it applied to any entertainment company or movie studio with a market capitalization above $150 billion. However, Disney, despite not being named, was clearly the target as the only primarily content company with copyright assets covered by the designated industry classification categories named in the bill — unless its market cap were suddenly to plummet. This was too cute by half. Hawley may as well have said that the legislation applied to any company that owned intellectual property in an anthropomorphic mouse that whistles. Hawley's draft legislation was bad law and terrible public policy. It went nowhere because the U.S. House of Representatives was not going to change the law to target just one company and retroactively expropriate its assets just because one senator happened not to like it. Apart from the legal challenges this would have entailed, the move reeked of political gamesmanship. Would it be fair comment to say the whole thing was just plain "Goofy"?

Banks and Jordan, and then Hawley, dredged up the issue as a stick with which to beat Disney because copyright protection on the first Mickey Mouse cartoon ever produced, "Steamboat Willie," which came out in 1928, will expire in the U.S. on January 1, 2024. On that date, the black-and-white sound cartoon in which a very different-looking Mickey from the one today, a Mickey who whistles but does not speak, will fall into the public domain. But Disney will retain copyright over all iterations of Mickey beyond this early cinematographic work and furthermore holds trademark rights over all uses of Mickey on a full range of products and merchandise as long as the marks are used and renewed. Not only that, this is not just about Mickey; the copyright on a lot of other works will also expire on the same day. This is a regular occurrence, a fact that anti-copyright crusaders try to exploit each year by proclaiming "Public Domain Day." This is just a publicity stunt to promote an anti-copyright agenda, suggesting that works under copyright protection have been locked away from the public for decades and are now suddenly liberated. This is nonsense.

In Canada, the copyright term was adjusted late in 2022 to life of the author plus seventy years, to match the term for the EU, Australia, Japan, and many other countries as well as for newer works in the U.S. Because of the history of copyright legislation in the U.S., where there were different (renewable) terms at different times, when Congress updated U.S. copyright law in 1976, it provided a period of protection for older works of seventy-five years from the date of the publication of the work, rather than tying the term to the lifespan of the author. For works published after January 1, 1978, a term of life plus fifty was legislated. In 1998, this term was extended by twenty years to bring the U.S. copyright term into alignment with that of the EU, whose term had become life plus seventy. At the same time, Congress also extended the period of seventy-five years from publication for older works by twenty years to ninety-five years.

At that time, the seventy-five-year copyright term for "Steamboat Willie" was nearing expiration, leading to a campaign by those opposed to term extension to identify the U.S. Copyright Term Extension Act of 1998 as the "Mickey Mouse Protection Act." While unfair and misleading, the label was used to mobilize anti-copyright elements to try to paint the legislation as a gift to one company. Although Disney, as a major copyright stakeholder, actively promoted extension (as did many other companies, associations, and groups with copyright interests), the main motivation for the legislation was to enable U.S. copyright holders to access the additional twenty years of copyright protection offered by the countries of the European Union. The U.S. Supreme Court, in dismissing a challenge (Eldred v Ashcroft) against the term extension, stated, "By extending the baseline United States copyright term to life plus seventy years, Congress sought to ensure that American authors would receive the same copyright protection in Europe as their European counterparts."[21]

The EU has a provision known as the "rule of the shorter term" whereby EU member states will not provide the full

21   Eric Eldred et al v John Ashcroft, Attorney-General, Supreme Court of the United States, January 15, 2003; https://www.copyright.gov/docs /eldrdedo.pdf; accessed November 3, 2022.

life plus seventy term of protection to authors from other countries unless EU copyright holders are given equivalent protection. In other words, the EU applies the principle of reciprocity to the extended term, as is its right under the Berne Convention. To avoid discriminatory treatment against U.S. copyright holders in the EU, the United States needed to provide the same level of protection to EU copyright holders as they enjoyed in their home market by extending its term, a provision that would of course be applicable to domestic copyright holders as well.

In 1993, the EU had implemented an extended term of life plus seventy through its copyright directive — applicable to all members — primarily in order to harmonize the term of protection among member states, which were of varying lengths. For example, Germany had a term of life plus seventy whereas Italy was life plus fifty-six, resulting in confusion about what works were protected by copyright within the EU. One stated reason for extending the term of protection was that originally the life plus fifty standard incorporated into the Berne Convention of 1886 was intended to protect works for two generations after the demise of the author. With longer life spans in the last decade of the twentieth century, a period of seventy years was now required to provide the equivalent level of protection. This was one justification (there were others), but the prime motivation was to harmonize the level of protection across all the member states. While internal consistency was the major factor for the EU, the result was that other countries not meeting the EU standard would find their copyright holders at a disadvantage in the EU market.

Once it had extended its term across all member states, the EU adopted reciprocity (or the rule of the shorter term) to encourage other countries to give equivalent protection to EU copyright holders abroad. In the case of the U.S., it worked. When Congress passed the Term Extension Act in 1998,[22] Disney was a beneficiary along with any other copyright holder whose work had not yet entered the public domain in the United States. While some countries have longer terms of protection than the U.S. or the EU (Mexico, for example, has a term of copyright protection of life plus one hundred — maybe people live longer in Mexico), there is no push in the U.S. or EU for extending the present term of copyright. Today, the focus is on encouraging those countries where the term of protection is only life plus fifty to align their terms of protection with those of most other developed nations. Canada committed to making this change as a result of trade agreement commitments, not in response to advocacy from the writing and publishing industry, a move that achieved the additional benefit of securing longer protection for our copyright holders in the EU, just as American copyright holders benefited once Congress adopted the Copyright Term Extension Act in 1998.

---

22 s-505, "Sonny Bono Copyright Term Extension Act," United States Congress, October 10, 1998; https://www.congress.gov/bill/105th-congress /senate-bill/505; accessed November 3, 2022.

Given the background to U.S. copyright extension twenty-five years ago and the current state of U.S. copyright law, it is frankly laughable to suggest that a movement to further extend the term of copyright protection in the United States would suddenly emerge, driven by the Walt Disney Company or anyone else. If there is no such movement, there is no need to publicly oppose it. This was all about political grandstanding, but that grandstanding would have had a lot more credibility if it had been based on facts and sound legal principles rather than a myth.

Selected Readings and References

Alford, William P. *To Steal a Book is an Elegant Offense: Intellectual Property Law in Chinese Civilization*. Stanford: Stanford University Press, 1995.

Bannerman, Sara. *The Struggle for Canadian Copyright: Imperialism to Internationalism 1842–1971*. Vancouver: UBC Press 2013.

Devine, Kyle. *Decomposed: The Political Ecology of Music*. Cambridge: MIT Press, 2019.

Finger, J. Michael and Philip Schuler (eds). *Poor People's Knowledge: Promoting Intellectual Property in Developing Countries*. Washington: World Bank and Oxford University Press, 2004.

Frankel, Suzy and Daniel J. Gervais. *Advanced Introduction to International Intellectual Property*. Cheltenham: Edward Elgar, 2016.

Gervais, Daniel J. *(Re)Structuring Copyright; A Comprehensive Path to International Copyright Reform*. Cheltenham: Edward Elgar, 2017.

Harris, Lesley Ellen. *Canadian Copyright Law (Fourth Edition)*. Hoboken: John Wiley & Sons, 2014.

Johns, Adrian. *Piracy: The Intellectual Property Wars from Gutenberg to Gates*. Chicago: University of Chicago Press, 2009, paperback edition 2011.

MacLaren, Eli. *Dominion and Agency: Copyright and the Structuring of the Canadian Book Trade, 1867–1918*. Toronto: University of Toronto Press, 2011.

Parliament of Canada, House of Commons. "Shifting Paradigms: Report of the Standing Committee on Canadian Heritage." May 2019, https://www.ourcommons.ca/DocumentViewer/en/42-1/CHPC/report-19/.

Parliament of Canada, House of Commons. "Statutory Review of the Copyright Act: Report of the Standing Committee on Industry, Science and Technology." June 2019, https://www.ourcommons.ca/DocumentViewer/en/42-1/INDU/report-16/.

Seville, Catherine. *The Internationalisation of Copyright Law: Books, Buccaneers and the Black Flag in the Nineteenth Century*. Cambridge: Cambridge University Press, 2006.

Slauter, Will. *Who Owns the News? A History of Copyright* Stanford: Stanford University Press, 2019.

Sookman, Barry, Carys Craig, and Steve Mason. *Copyright: Cases and Commentary on the Canadian and International Law, Second Edition*. Toronto: Carswell, 2014.

Vats, Anjali. *The Color of Creatorship: Intellectual Property, Race and the Making of Americans*. Stanford: Stanford University Press, 2020.

Wang, Fei-Hsien. *Pirates and Publishers: A Social History of Copyright in Modern China*. Princeton: Princeton University Press, 2019.

Acknowledgements

I would like to acknowledge Marc Côté, the publisher of Cormorant Books, without whose vision and support this book would not have been written. Marc saw the need for the book and encouraged me to take it on. Without him and the capable staff at Cormorant, the project would not have been completed.

I am also grateful for the intellectual support and inspiration provided over the years by a dedicated group of copyright bloggers — Neil Turkewitz, David Newhoff, and Stephen Carlisle — as well as Keith Kupferschmidt, Eileen Bramlet, and others at the Copyright Alliance. None of this group, however, reviewed the content of the book. It follows, therefore, that any errors or omissions must be attributed solely to me.

Best known for his blog *Insights on International Copyright Issues* (awarded one of the top copyright blogs in the world and consistently ranked by Feedspot as a Top 50 copyright blog) Hugh Stephens has written articles for the Canadian Global Affairs Institute, *The Globe and Mail*, the *National Post, The Conversation, The Diplomat,* and more. He served for several years as Vice Chair of the Quality Brands Protection Committee, a coalition of more than 180 multinational companies engaged in strengthening IPR protection in China. Stephens was educated at the University of British Columbia (UBC), University of Toronto and Duke University, and has a Certificate in Mandarin from the Chinese University of Hong Kong. He is also a Distinguished Fellow at the Asia Pacific Foundation of Canada, Executive Fellow at the School of Public Policy at the University of Calgary, and an associate faculty member in the School of Business at Royal Roads University in Victoria, BC, where he is currently based.

We acknowledge the sacred land on which Cormorant Books operates. It has been a site of human activity for 15,000 years. This land is the territory of the Huron-Wendat and Petun First Nations, the Seneca, and most recently, the Mississaugas of the Credit River. The territory was the subject of the Dish With One Spoon Wampum Belt Covenant, an agreement between the Iroquois Confederacy and Confederacy of the Ojibway and allied nations to peaceably share and steward the resources around the Great Lakes. Today, the meeting place of Toronto is still home to many Indigenous people from across Turtle Island. We are grateful to have the opportunity to work in the community, on this territory.

We are also mindful of broken covenants and the need to strive to make right with all our relations.